Fame Sex Money Power

Fame Sex Money Power

A Beginner's Guide

edited by

CRAIG de BROWN

CHATTO & WINDUS
LONDON

TO THE BEAUFORTS —
MOSH, MARY, GILES AND SAM

Published in 1987 by
Chatto & Windus Ltd
30 Bedford Square
London WC1B 3RP

British Library Cataloguing in Publication Data

Fame sex money power: a beginner's guide.
1. Success – Anecdotes, facetiae, satire etc.
I. Brown, Craig
158′.1′0207   BF637.S8

ISBN 0-7011-3190-X

Designed by Roger Lightfoot

Typeset by Columns of Reading
Printed in Great Britain by
Redwood Burn Ltd, Trowbridge, Wiltshire

INTRODUCTION

Go-getting car magnate John de Lorean.
Wealthy philosopher Edward de Bono.
Petite songbird Lyndsey de Paul.
Millionaire pop manager Tony de Freis.
Respected tycoon Peter de Savary.
International fashion celebrity Justin de Villeneuve.
They all have just one thing in common.
THEY MADE IT.
They went out and grabbed it and having grabbed it they kept it.
My kind of people.
Your kind of people.
Their own kind of people.
SO HOW DID THEY DO IT?
They wouldn't tell me.
What would they stand to gain from spilling the beans?
ZERO.

LESSON ONE: TOP PEOPLE DON'T GO BLEATING TO TIDDLERS.

Only out-and-out idiots would want to share their secrets of success with the general reader. So I'm especially grateful to all those who have contributed to this book. With their advice you'll be able to go anywhere, do anything, and make a million. ZANY philosopher Ambrose de Solaire. Super-rich POLITICIAN Sir Shortley de Peverill. SEXY and SYMPATHETIC fitness expert Penny de Rennie. CONGENIAL man of letters Sir Harvey de Marlowe. SUCCESSFUL entrepreneur Terence de Brittish. Well-Known MAN ABOUT

TOWN Chris P. Rice. LEADING BROADCASTER Stewart de Stuart. Upfront SOCIALITE Lady Eva de Topliss.
All of them BOLD.
DYNAMIC.
FORCEFUL.
And above all SUCCESSFUL.
All of them much better people than you.
But, armed with FAME SEX MONEY POWER, you too can BE LIKE THEM.

WARNING: THIS BOOK WILL CHANGE YOUR LIFE

Craig de Brown

Editor

Name

Sir Harvey de Marlowe

Date of birth

5 April 1915

Profession

Author, critic, publisher, biographer, écriviste, broadcaster, man of letters, bon viveur.

Position currently held

Fellow of the Worshipful Company of Authors; regular contributor to *Arts Aplenty* with Melvyn Bragg; Managing Director, Wildbore House publishers (authors include Steve Cram, Delia Smith, Dennis Norden, etc.); judge, Booker Prize 1988.

Family

Of little interest to the general reader.

Achievements to date

Publications: *Bloomsbury: The Memory Lingers*, 1961; *A Short Walk in Hyde Park* (travel), 1963; *The Oxford Book of Bits and Pieces* (editor), 1966; *The Oscar Wilde I Never Knew* (biography), 1970; *Bloomsbury: And Still the Memory Lingers*, 1972; *Armchair India* (travel), 1975; *A Literary Sort of Chap* (autobiography), 1979; *The Wit of Paul Johnson* (editor), 1982; *The Marsh–Marlowe Letters*, 1984; *Bloomsbury: A Time to Recall*, 1986; (in preparation) *The Oxford Book of Unmemorable Verse*.

Awards

Knighted for Services to Literature, 1971. Many dinners at Clarence House.

High point of career

Partaking of luncheon with Sir Laurens van der Post, Savoy Grill, 1986.

Low point of career

Failing to recognise the early genius of Melvyn Bragg, who is now, I'm pleased to relate, a good friend.

Best friend

Paul Johnson, Roy Hattersley, Melvyn Bragg, Gerald Marsh (old schoolmaster), Frederic Raphael, Lady Eva de Topliss.

What makes you happy

Civilised conversation; a good cut of beef; a well-written book; perusing *The Spectator*; dinner with close friends; a decent pudding; a cigar to follow.

What makes you sad

'Modern' things, including 'feminists', the Good News Bible, teaching homosexuality to children, anti-racism lobbies, motorways, the National Health Service, the destruction of the old county names, the Series 3 liturgy, and Brahms' Requiem.

What qualities do you look for in a human being

A sense of humour. Values. Well-readness.

Most memorable disaster

On receiving my knighthood from Her Majesty, she asked me what my favourite book was. For an awful moment my mind went blank: I could remember no book ever written. 'My Mind's Gone Blank, ma'am,' I said. 'Oh yes,' she replied, 'I haven't read it myself but I'm told it's awfully good.'

Heroes

James Lees-Milne; Sir Laurens van der Post; Dr Johnson; most definitely NOT Jon Pilger or Emily Pankhurst.

Ambitions

To cook the perfect soufflé. To write the perfect line. Both very similar ambitions in their way.

If you weren't yourself who would you choose to be

Someone who knew me.

Pets if any

A golden retriever called Flaubert.

Hobbies

Writing, eating and talking: if possible, all at the same time.

Religious convictions if any

I believe in the Tridentine Mass, in the preservation of old country churches without electric guitar and banjo services conducted by long-haired 'black' vicars, and with the Church keeping its nose out of politics.

Favourite book

Melvyn Bragg's autobiography, *I Bragg*.

If you had three wishes what would they be

1. To write with the admirable fluency of Godfrey Smith.
2. To be as witty as Frederic Raphael.
3. To look like Dr Roy Strong.

What would you most like to be remembered for

Championing first-time novelists is always the delight and privilege of a publisher: I think now of Claire Francis, Jill Tweedie and John Kennedy O'Toole, to all of whom I gave a leg-up.

Pet hate

'Experimental' novels; 'modern' jazz; 'trendy' vicars, 'free' verse.

Favourite catchphrase

I'm rather above all that.

Are you frightened of death and if so why

I remember asking William Golding precisely the same question over a luncheon of quenelles and strawberry soufflé at the Caprice in 1961. He looked at me with that wise expression, took another sip of Chablis, stroked his beard for a second, and then replied, but I forget exactly what he said.

'Ploughing a Rut in a Sea of Letters'

SIR HARVEY DE MARLOWE, FWCA

Writing is a craft like any other. You've got to work at making your sentences pithy, intelligent and above all elegant – and work hard.

There is, however, nothing more satisfying than a successful career in the world of letters. In a long and varied life, I have never made the distinction, as many do, between writer and critic, or critic and publisher, or publisher and journalist. For me they go together like eggs, bacon, four sausages and a nice fat slice of fried bread, make that two. We're all dealing in the commodity called *WORDS*. Words are the bread and butter of writing; without *WORDS* there's nowhere to put the jam.

So what are these strange appliances called *WORDS*, and how does one go about selecting the right ones?

First you must ask yourself: What meaning do I wish to convey?

Obviously, this will differ from writer to writer and from sentence to sentence. I doubt very much whether one of our leftist writer friends would wish to convey the same meaning in his sentence as a more fair-minded, logical fellow such as Paul Johnson. So the first essential of any successful sentence is *MEANING*.

MEANING: AVOID MAKING IT UNCLEAR

Let us say that you wish to call for a return to Capital Punishment. How do you go about it? (I'm talking now of composing the sentence, of course, not Capital Punishment, which one goes about by pulling a lever, I believe!)

Now it may well be that you come to the decision before picking up your fountain pen that the arguments in support of Capital Punishment are so first-class and that there are so many of 'em that you might need two or even three sentences to bring out the whole of your *MEANING*. Fair enough. Paul Johnson once said that there was nothing worth saying that couldn't be said in three well-chosen words, but few of us can equal his almost magical ability with the English language, so I think that, for the purposes of this lesson at least, we should allow ourselves three sentences. This amounts to an *Argument*: a *statement* progressing with *logic* towards a *conclusion*. In the first sentence, concentrate on the *statement*:

SENTENCE ONE: It is wrong to kill.

Excellent! With five simple words, you have made your position crystal clear. Few people in their right minds could argue with you over that one. Now to the next step, *logic*:

SENTENCE TWO: People who kill are wrong.

Again, five words, all logical, all progressing to the conclusion:

SENTENCE THREE: Therefore
(– *the word 'therefore' is a great help to all writers*)
Therefore, wrong people must be killed.

Delicious! You are now a writer and will be able to gain employment penning 'think pieces' for any of our national tabloids.

Do not worry if you have few opinions at the start. This handy checklist of suitable opinions more or less covers every topic. It is the very same checklist used by top Fleet Street writers Paul Johnson, Lynda Lee-Potter, George Gale and Geoffrey Wheatcroft before they sit down for a hard half hour of writing.

Do not worry if you do not possess many thoughts; you can use this to great advantage. For as long as anyone can remember, there have only ever been twenty-five worthwhile opinions and these benefit greatly from healthy repetition.

25 Frank and Fearless Opinions to Hold –
The Official Checklist
PLEASE CARRY THIS LIST ABOUT
YOUR PERSON AT ALL TIMES

Social Issues

This rising tide of violence which threatens to engulf
us
This rising tide of drugs which threatens to engulf
us
This rising tide of immigrants which threatens to
engulf us
This rising tide of promiscuity which threatens to
engulf us
This rising tide of obscenity which threatens to
engulf us

Political Issues

The creeping menace of the loony left hell-bent on
power
The creeping menace of hunt saboteurs hell-bent on
power
The creeping menace of anti-nuclear campaigners
hell-bent on power
The creeping menace of so-called 'democrats'
hell-bent on power
The creeping menace of anti-racists hell-bent on
power

History

Our Fairy-tale Princess
Our Fairy-tale Prince
Our Fairy-tale Queen Mum
Our Fairy-tale Queen
Our no-nonsense Prince Philip

Britain

Our British bobby – despite everything, still the best
in the world
Our television – despite everything, still the best in
the world
Our Parliament – despite everything, still the best in
the world
Our countryside – despite everything, still the best
in the world
Our cities – despite everything, still the best in the
world

Whatever Happened To?

Whatever happened to the old half-crown?
Whatever happened to freedom of speech?
Whatever happened to that old-fashioned word
respect?
Whatever happened to law and order?
Whatever happened to tunes you could hum?

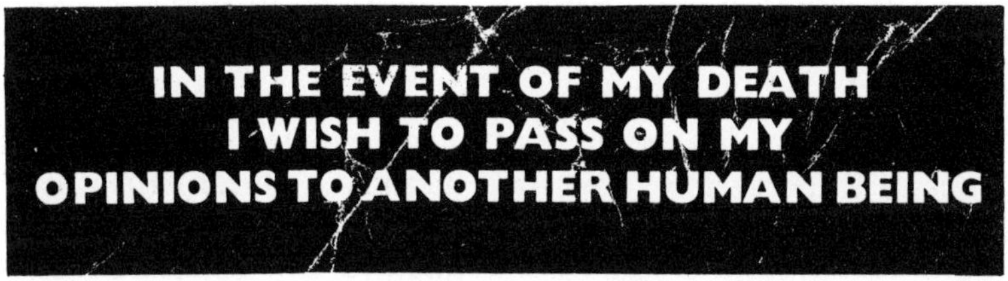

IN THE EVENT OF MY DEATH
I WISH TO PASS ON MY
OPINIONS TO ANOTHER HUMAN BEING

Fig. 1 An opinion-donor card. Many top journalists such as Paul Johnson
keep these cards about their person at all times.

All Fleet Street's accredited opinion-formers – among them Lynda Lee-Potter, Paul Johnson and that perennial jester Auberon Waugh – carry this official checklist of acceptable opinions about their person *at all times*. In the event of a car crash or similar personal tragedy, they can then pass on their opinions, giving a full and rich life in journalism to another human being.

A lot of twaddle is spoken in the leftist and subversive press about the 'interference' of press proprietors. Nothing, in my experience, could be further from the truth. Ten years ago, I was lucky enough to publish the first authorised critical biography of Robert Maxwell, the highly successful proprietor of the *Daily Mirror*. The biography, *Big-Hearted Bob* (Pergamon Press, £15.95) showed the world in touching detail the private man behind the 'tycoon' façade, a man who once gave ten pence to a busker in the street at a very advantageous rate of interest, a man who is able to say of himself, 'I'd speak to a king or a pauper in just the same manner. Unless the pauper was making a nuisance of himself.'

The same is true of Rupert Murdoch, a charming and gentle man whose earliest ambition was to enter an enclosed order. 'Just imagine the headline,' he once said to me, ' "Naughty Monks in Sex Frolics" – we'd add on a hundred thou overnight!'

It is a little-known fact that every single one of those journalists into whose hands has come the Checklist on page 14 has, within the space of six months, been asked to dine with Rupert Murdoch at his private table at the Ritz.

How should I Behave Over Dinner at the Ritz with Rupert Murdoch?

'You can tell a lot about a guy by the way he eats his nosebag' is one of Rupert's most treasured dictums. A meal with Rupert is in fact an 'audition' to become one of his leading executives or star columnists. These are the qualities for which he will be searching as you eat:
a) Drive
b) Push
c) Go
d) Thrust
e) Pull

Roy Hattersley's Writing Course

Lesson 29: The Light Touch

People often tell me how amusing my occasional essays are. I certainly like to think that I have the 'light touch'. What do I mean when I say that I have the 'light touch'? This is an exceptionally good question and one that I shall now endeavour to place an answer to.

Let us take a simple point of view. Let us say, for reasons of argument, that it is 'I am Roy Hattersley'. This is, as it happens, the recurrent theme that can be detected in all my occasional essays. Someone without the light touch might simply write 'I am Roy Hattersley' and leave it at that. But, I would argue, there is nothing in that sentence, for all its qualities of brevity, to amuse the reader. So let's see how that very same sentence looks after it has been passed through what I call 'The Hattersley Wordmill'.

My most sympathetic of readers may well come to appreciate that, for good or ill, I, ebullient as ever, am – and many readers have written in to confirm me in this somewhat forthright point of view – the very same man who was christened 'Roy', an appellation to which I can think of no earthly reason to object, and whose surname is the similarly pleasing and not wholly undistinguished 'Hattersley' – touché!

This is what is known as the light touch.

Next issue:
Lesson 30: Letting the reader know that you are well read.

He has no time for shilly-shallyers. 'No one got anywhere listening to the other point of view,' is the message he has pinned above his shaving mirror. Throughout dinner, the aspirant executive must be assertive and forthright, without ever expressing a contrary view.

6.45pm. Meet in Palm Court, Ritz Hotel.
Rupert offers big, strong handshake. While shaking your hand, he will look hard into your eyes. *Be careful not to show him any tears.*
FIRST QUESTION:
R.M.: What're you drinking?
DON'T SAY:
You: Oh, dear, I'm told it's rather expensive in this place.
SHOUT ASSERTIVELY:
You: Lager – and keep it in the bloody can!

7.10. SECOND QUESTION:
R.M.: D'you fancy another before dinner?
DON'T SAY:
You: Well, that might be nice, but let me pay this time.
SHOUT ASSERTIVELY:
You: Not on your bloody nelly! I like to keep a clear head at all times!

7.11. Before dinner, Rupert likes to ask an apparently casual question, often related to your personal well-being, family, films seen, etc. In fact, it is a big question in disguise.
FIRST BIG QUESTION:
R.M.: I forget, are you married at all?
DON'T SAY:
You: Yes, I have a wife, Jane, and two little daughters, Emily, five, and Rebecca who'll be three this June.
SHOUT ASSERTIVELY:
You: She's a super-summer scorcher with the kind of figure that makes most blokes' hearts miss a beat, a sizzling pair of legs and a firm commitment to traditional values!

7.15. R.M. leads you to his private table in the Marie Antoinette Room. *Ignore* the telex, word-processor, computer compositor and secretaries stationed behind wine-cooler. Look at the menu for *no more than three seconds* before deciding.
SECOND BIG QUESTION:
R.M.: Did you catch the news today?
DON'T SAY:

You: Yes – *The Times* led on the threat of sanctions to Nicaragua whilst the *Guardian* concentrated its attention on the growing trade deficit of the Common Market countries.

SHOUT ASSERTIVELY:

You: Brrr! It's a freeze-up! But as the rest of the country shivers, sexy Sam shows her charms in this skimpy Santa outfit. Betcha wouldn't mind this Christmas sizzler dropping down your chimneys, eh, fellas?!!!!

7.25.   The waiter arrives to take your order.

DON'T SAY:

You: What do you particularly recommend off today's menu, please?

SHOUT ASSERTIVELY:

You: Chicken with all the trimmings and all the gravy you can manage!

When the waiter says: 'Will you be starting with anything, sir?'

DON'T SAY:

You: Actually, I'm on a diet, but I might manage a little tomato soup.

SHOUT ASSERTIVELY:

You: I've already said I'm having the *chicken*, dumbo, and I'll have the same again for main.

7.35.   The food is brought to your table. Eat it with *drive* and *ambition*, without recourse to knife and fork.

7.36.   When you have downed the fowl:

DON'T SAY:

You: Mmmm, that was delicious.

BURP ASSERTIVELY

7.37.   When you have downed the next fowl, do likewise. Having passed all the tests so far, you enter the time allotted for Business Discussions.

THIRD BIG QUESTION:

7.40.   R.M.: I'll tell you frankly, I'm very keen to have you working for my organisation. I've been a great admirer of your stuff for a long time now. Which job could I tempt you with?

DON'T SAY:

You: I'd like to be in a position, perhaps as third leader writer on *The Times*, where I can put forward broadly Conservative-based views in a cogent and far-sighted manner.

SHOUT ASSERTIVELY:

You: Chief Murders Reporter on the *News of the World!* With increasing cross-fertilisation of News International newspapers, it will be possible for the right man to hold both these posts – *Times*/Leaders and *NoW*/Murders – simultaneously with a correspondingly adjusted salary increase.

7.45.   Leavetaking.

R.M.: Welcome to the Organisation. Nice to have working for us a man with a mind of my own.

R.M. delivers punch to shoulder. Looks hard into your eyes. Remember: *show no tears*.

High-action Adventure Thriller Writing

No one writes novels quite like Jeffrey Archer, an author for whom I have immense respect. Those of us who have attended his splendid Wednesday celebrity luncheons have nothing but praise for the writing skills of this consummate man of our times who has, in his own words, 'been to hell and back – to emerge the world's number one writer. Not bad for a guy who once owed half a million. Shall I give you the whole story, it'll undoubtedly interest your readers . . .'

Not for Jeffrey the murky rooting about in the muddy backwaters of pseudo-psychology. 'I always say if you dive deep you'll come up filthy,' he always says. 'I'm all for giving the ordinary common-or-garden reader what he wants – a bloody good yarn with a beginning, a middle and an end – and preferably in that order!!'

His books, as we all know, are red-hot bestsellers. They make it impossible to stop turning the pages – even when you want to read them!

THE WRITER'S HANDBOOK

Ten Handy Tips from the Word-Processor of Jeffrey Archer

1) *Know Your Stuff*

I always say there's no point writing if you don't know your stuff. Research is the name of the game. If your hero wears shoes, then you should wear shoes too, to get the feel of what it's like. Readers love the telling detail. For instance, that the Russian secret police are called the 'KGB' and that their counterparts in America are called the 'CIA'. For my last book, I spent months discovering telling details such as the name of the current President of America, the address of the White House – that's the building in Washington where the President is known to live, the exact location of Moscow – that's the capital of Russia, a fact our communist friends would rather we didn't know, the way in which the highly-complex '24-hour-clock' system of time-keeping operates (my children, whom I count among my greatest fans, are proud to tell their private-schoolfriends that their father is one of the few men in this country to have mastered the 24-hour-clock system of time-keeping), the quickest route from Trafalgar Square to Buckingham Palace in a car travelling at eighty hours per mile.

All these little details let readers feel, smell and taste your characters – and those books will sell, sell, sell.

2) *Grip the Reader*
What does a reader want from a book?

I'll tell you for free.

Action. In a nutshell.

Your average reader's not the slightest bit interested in fine prose, lengthy descriptions of the countryside, poetic insights into the nature of the human condition or – my big turn-off, I can tell you – journeys into the heart of man. He wants guns, chases, romantic interest and exotic locations. He wants fast cars, fast birds and fast money. Let's face it, he wants a damn good read.

And it's my job to give it to him.

Judging by my latest sales figures – 50 billion worldwide – it's not a job I do too badly.

But things weren't always like that, I can tell you. I've been to hell and back – and won.

3) *Get that First Sentence Right*
– 'Damn your bloody guts,' said Fraser, the gun still smouldering.
– 'To kill fifty VIPs in the space of five hours,' snarled Jackson, 'that's your task, Hamilton.'

- 'I've just about had all I can take of this,' barked Maxwell while the blood spurted out of the fifty-three bullet holes in his chest.
- All happy families resemble one another, each unhappy family is unhappy in its own way.
- 'I'll kill anything that moves,' said KGB double-agent Yuri Yurimov, the torchlight sparkling in his two false eyes.

Four of the above quotations are first sentences from four of my internationally bestselling novels. The other I have stolen from a dusty old tome you'd be hard-pressed to find on the shelves of even the stuffiest airport bookstall. It doesn't take me to tell you which is the great turn-off: it's number four. The air-traveller these days doesn't want to be plunged into gloom and despondency as he fastens his safety belt. He wants to be gripped by the lapels and hurtled through a hurly-burly world of international intrigue and personal survival so that, when he emerges a few hours later at a foreign airport, his business acumen is refreshed and he can sign up a deal that is good for him, good for his company and, above all, good for Britain.

4) *Get that Last Sentence Right*
After 350-odd pages of fast-moving adventure, your average reader is keen to be left with something to chew on, some little thought or *pensée*, as our friends over the Channel (incidentally, some of my most devoted fans are French) would have it. Having got his girl, shot his way to freedom and found what he was looking for, our hero should stand back for the last sentence of the book and have a bloody good think. I've always been philosophical by nature – you'd have to be if you'd been faced with debts of half a million and worked your way back from the brink of disaster within just three years! – and I like to give my readers some of the benefit of my thoughts. But these should always be restricted to the very last sentence – no reader wants too much of a good thing. Let's take a look at what I'm talking about.

These are the last sentences from my four bestselling blockbusters:
- 'Funny old world,' thought Fraser, throwing down his automatic.

- Hamilton looked steely. 'I guess there are some things in this life we're just not meant to know,' he said thoughtfully.
- 'I've been thinking,' exclaimed Maxwell as her blue eyes stared at him longingly. 'Two and two don't always make four, you know.'
- The corpse of Yurimov at last lay at his feet, a grotesque rag doll, useless and outworn. Burton thought long and hard. 'The past is in the past – we must live for the present – and for the future as well.'

Have you noticed that the verb 'to think' is common to each of the above passages? That's because I'm a thinking sort of guy – and I think my readers are too. *But let's keep that thought to the last sentence, shall we?*

5) *Keep them Guessing*
Critics are constantly describing my books as 'unputdownable'. You want to know what'll happen next. And the same cannot be said of some of our more 'highbrow' authors whose combined sales figures couldn't keep me in hot dinners but who somehow manage to have a monopoly on the attention of our more elitist reviewers, who are themselves in the pay of the leftist Arts Council supremos.

Here's a chapter plan for my next novel but one, *A Shot in the Arm,* which, you may well be interested to hear, has already earned me a pre-publication advance of over 60 million – that's *million* – pounds: and this for a man who once faced debts of over £600,000! Makes you think!

Note how in each separate chapter the story moves on and a new question of 'what'll happen next' prompts the reader to keep turning them pages – and that's the true motive of any novelist, whether he's Shakespeare or Arthur Miller, the American who was once married to Marilyn Monroe.

Chapter One: First sentence – 'There was nothing Mason wouldn't do to gain his first million pounds. "There's nothing I wouldn't do to gain my first million pounds," he said icily. And that was what he set out to do – gain his first million pounds. And there was nothing he wouldn't do to gain it.'

Further establish Mason's character – ambitious, ruthless. How will he go about gaining his million?

Chapter Two: Introduction of Mason's rival, Hopkirk.
Hopkirk's character – ruthless, ambitious. Introduction of Hopkirk's wild ambition: 'There was nothing Hopkirk wouldn't do to gain his first million pounds.'
How will Hopkirk go about it?

Chapter Three: More on Mason's early years. Born in Leningrad – show research on Leningrad (lots of houses, citizens Russian, chilly in winter, vodka drunk). Poor family. Mother killed by ruthless tyrant. Mason vows revenge – and means to get it.
How will Mason gain revenge on his mother's killer?

Chapter Four: More on Hopkirk's early years. Born in Africa – show research on Africa (few houses, citizens mainly black and African, giraffes in bush, scorching sun, uprisings). Rich family. Father kills woman in Leningrad. Hopkirk vows to kill orphan before orphan kills him.
Who is the orphan?

Chapter Five: Back to Mason. Through sheer drive and ruthless ambition Mason drags himself up out of the hell-hole that is Leningrad and in a series of adventures including time in prison (research: prison dark and damp) he escapes, becomes international businessman, makes a million. Buys gun. Sets off to kill son of mother's killer.
Who is the son of his mother's killer?

Chapter Six: Back to Hopkirk. Through sheer drive and ruthless ambition Hopkirk becomes king of African state, is overthrown in uprising and in a series of adventures including time on board ship (research: ships often involved in storms) he escapes, penniless, becomes international businessman, makes million. Buys gun. Finds out name of orphan he must kill – man of his own age called . . . Mason!

Chapter Seven: Penthouse suite in New York (research: busy, skyscrapers). Mason prepares to meet new client for business deal. The client's name is . . . Hopkirk! At last!
Who will win in this intense battle of wits?

Chapter Eight: 'You!' say both Hopkirk and Mason simultaneously. After fierce recriminations, each pulls out his gun at the same time and shoots the other stone dead. Their respective secretaries enter at the same time, screaming. They see each other. 'Karen!' they both say at

'Let Me Tell You a Story'
Archer's Catch-All Anecdote Chart

STAGE 1	2	3	4	5

That reminds me, Libby, of a lovely story that relates to my current bestseller, *A Shot in the Arm*. One day, my

wife — came up to me and said, 'Daddy/Darling, we love you so much, why do you have to put so much time into researching your bestselling books?'

youngest child

oldest child — ran up to me and said, 'Daddy/Darling, how do you manage to write so many terrific bestsellers like your latest, *A Shot in the Arm*?'

to which I replied

'I care for my readers, and if they're going to have the great read they require then I owe it to them to do my homework.'

'You know, you wouldn't have a bestselling author for a daddy/husband if he didn't write bestsellers ha ha,' rather sweet I thought.

'If I knew how I wouldn't have to devote so much time to researching my next bestseller after the latest, *A Shot in the Arm* ha ha.' And I think there's a certain amount of truth in that, don't you, Libby?

'I certainly can't stop now, lovey, as I well remember the day I got a bill for half a million dropped through my letter box!'

once. It emerges that – through sheer coincidence – they are long-lost sisters, both called Karen.

Last sentence: 'The sisters' tears of joy as they hugged over the dead bodies of their former employers were a testament to the way in which good can so often come out of bad. "So often," said Karen, "out of bad can come good."'

THE END

6) *Go Out and Sell That Book*

I've heard of one or two authors who think they're somehow 'above' the marketplace. Well, let me tell you, no one's above the marketplace, because a book is a product like a Hoover or a washing machine. I always think of my own books as face-flannels, and my friends in the face-flannel game inform me that they go to great lengths to sell their face-flannels to the public in no uncertain terms. And they have to, because what's to stop Joe Public deserting his face-flannel for a sponge or just soap and cold water, my own particular favourite?

Point taken.

7) *Learn to Present Yourself*

I must have done over ten thousand interviews with press and television in my time, and along the way I've learned one hell of a lot about technique.

* Mention the title of the book every ten words.
* Mention the Christian name of the interviewer every twelve words. This makes him feel – temporarily – that he is on your level, and may well lead to extended interview time.
* Mention an amusing anecdote concerning your immediate family at least twice every five minutes: this aids reader-identification.
* Smile hard. A smile is performed by raising both edges of your mouth simultaneously. It helps if you are feeling pleased with yourself at the time.

As Jeffrey so rightly points out, these days those of us in the publishing game have at last outgrown the fuddy-duddy distinction between what is 'art' and what is not. Jeffrey's books move along at a cracking pace – something one could never say of a sculpture by, say, George Moore. I might add, in all modesty, that I was an early pioneer in bringing a ray of reality to book production. In the late 1960s, I was the first publisher to offer the public the lavishly produced new-style 'coffee table' books, throwing in four screw-on legs with each purchase, a scheme that has since caught on worldwide.

Literary Criticism

Those without the 'get-up-and-go' of a Jeffrey Archer might well consider becoming a Literary Critic. Frankly, in my long and fruitful career as a literary critic (incidentally, always a charming excuse for partaking of luncheon with some of our more civilised publishers!) I have always been struck by one golden rule, and that is never to review a book by someone I don't know. I have maintained this rule to an extent that others less – shall we say? – impartial than I no doubt deem to be absurdly uncompromising. I have acquaintances, not friends, but acquaintances, in the world of literary journalism who do not blanch at reviewing any book, even if they have never so much as exchanged smiles with its author. My old chum Godfrey Smith, whose literary column on the *Sunday Times* is notable for its lack of frosty bookishness, summed it up in the proverbial nutshell when he penned the following *pensée*:

Arf, arf, come off it, me hearties! Burppp! On my way back from a nigh on glorious repast with me old fellow guzzler and erstwhile colleague Bernard Levin, he of the silvery and inimitable prose, our delicious chat turns to books, arf, arf, those multi-paged tomes replete with well-chosen words and – fingers crossed! – pictures. Slurping a hefty suck of tiptop strawberry ice-lolly, I venture to suggest to pal Bernard that friend Will Shakespeare, the bard himself, forsooth, was one chap for whom I would pull up me chair and tuck into a tasty banquet, bard or no bard. Bernard, estimable word-smith that he is, plumped an added aperçu aboard the thought-trolley, namely that our merry jester of a bard will be remembered for his little beard and big heart long after the 'apless 'Amlet – he of the plodding problems – has been milked dry. That's yer portion this week, folks, arf! arf! Burppp!

The Eezi-Plan Christmas Review Chart

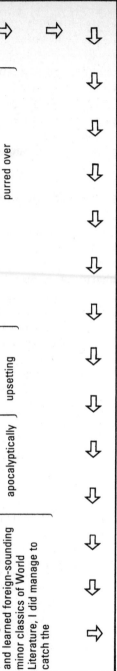

Opening phrase					
I have no hesitation in choosing the	infinitely	ferocious	TITLE	which I	perused
From a particularly rich crop, I finally go for the	deliciously	sensitive			lapped up
A disappointing year, saved for me by the	felicitously	moving			enjoyed
Though I spent most of the year engrossed in obscure and learned foreign-sounding minor classics of World Literature, I did manage to catch the	engagingly	hilarious			read from cover to cover
	charmingly	distinguished			managed to finish
	worryingly	learned			leaped upon
	apocalyptically	upsetting			purred over

with

take my hat off to

With this book, the author has once again proved himself among our

foremost chroniclers	
wittiest observers	
key historians	of
most telling commentators	
liveliest apologists	

inner-city · adolescent · childhood · working-class · fin-de-siècle · contemporary · post-nuclear · post-modernist · postmen's

angst. · enchantment. · experience. · experiment. · malaise. · disenchantment. · loss of faith. · goals and aspirations. · despair.

tears rolling down my cheeks. · mounting horror. · a great deal of pleasure. · numbing trepidation. · growing concentration. · civilised approbation. · glass in hand.

I

take my hat off to · salute · dine out with · raise my glass to · welcome · raise my left trouser leg for · greatly admire · owe · live with

this

sparkling talent. · original mind. · exquisite intellect. · personable écriviste. · outstanding bon viveur. · immense genius. · giant. · friend of mankind. · side-splitting fellow.

Heartily · Heavily · Happily · Highly

recommended.

Once you have got your friend's book to review, what next? Some would argue that it should be read, but I feel that this is taking what should, after all, be an essentially pleasurable pastime a mite too far. It is particularly unnecessary when it comes to selecting one's Book of the Year for the Christmas pages of the smarter newspapers – wonderfully palatable reading, in my op. Deft reference to the Eezi-Plan chart will save you a lot of time that might have been spent reading, as well as causing your best chum a considerable amount of well-heeled delight – cheers all round, without so much as a turn of a page.

Happy and prosperous scribbling!

A–Z of Book Reviews

A   **Authentic.** Barely decipherable.
B   **Beautifully intricate.** Didn't get to the end.
C   **Charming.** I've stayed with the author.
D   **Delightful.** I've stayed two nights with the author.
E   **Evocative.** Full of adjectives.
F   **First rate.** Third rate.
G   **Generous.** Uncritical.
H   **Hugely enjoyable.** Author's fat.
I   **Intensely personal.** Cookbook.
J   **Jolly.** Author's fat and stupid.
K   **Kiss and tell.** Met once and employed ghost-writer.
L   **Lavishly illustrated.** No text to speak of.
M   **Major.** Minor.
N   **Nostalgic.** Clichéd.
O   **Oozes with joie de vivre.** Author's monstrously fat and alcoholic.
P   **Perhaps** (*as in 'Perhaps the wittiest . . .'*). I haven't read the competition.
Q   **Quietly moving.** No pictures.
R   **Rare insight.** Employed a researcher for a fortnight.
S   **Sinuous.** I'm having an affair with the author.
T   **Thoughtful.** Long.
U   **Unique.** First this year.
V   **Versatile.** Has television series.
W   **Wry.** No exclamation marks.
X   **Xylyphozeretic.** Anthony Burgess reviewing.
Y   **Youthful.** I'm married to the author.
Z   **Zany.** Author wears tinted spectacles.

Name

Sir Shortley de Peverill, PC, OBE

Date of birth

January 4th, 1931

Profession

Company Director; Happily Married Man.

Position currently held

Honorary Treasurer, the Conservative Association for Disgraced Former Ministers.

Family

Wife Melissa, a trooper, and two children, both tragic.

Achievements to date

Publications: *It Wasn't My Fault* (autobiography, 1982). Frequent contributions to *Punch*, *High Life* and the *Sunday Express*.

Awards

Junior swimming and high jump, St Kildred's, 1940. Bronze medal, badminton, Marlborough College, 1946. Various golf trophies, St Swithin's Golfing Society, 1960–85. OBE, 1980. Runner-up, Pipe-smoker of the Year, 1984.

High point of career

Appointment as Junior Minister for Defence, 1980.

Low point of career

I can see little point in raking over the old ground that led to my voluntary resignation from my ministerial responsibilities in April 1981, and I am sure that the future holds many fresh challenges.

Best friend

I have the greatest respect for our Prime Minister, the Rt Hon. Margaret Thatcher, a woman of courage and vision. Also my wife Melissa who has stood by me.

What makes you happy

The feeling that I have something to offer my country.

What makes you sad

The increasing disregard among some sections of the population for the very real problems faced by our admirable police force; left-wing bias in the BBC.

What qualities do you look for in a human being

A sense of humour; guts; the sheer courage to say 'Stop that whining: I'm having none of it.'

Most memorable disaster

Once when visiting an unemployment centre I was mistaken for a member of the unemployed by one of the little people showing me around, but I laughed it off. Lucky for them their Minister was noted for his sense of humour!

Heroes

The Prime Minister; the bobby on the beat; our boys in the Falklands; Sir Winston Churchill; that great all-round family entertainer, Miss Cilla Black; the Royal Family, many of whom I have been privileged to meet personally; ordinary men and women in the street.

Ambitions

To increase the membership and influence of the Conservative Association for Disgraced Former Ministers. On a more personal level, to complete my first novel, a thriller with a twist.

If you weren't yourself who would you choose to be

An ordinary man or woman in the street.

Pets if any

Pedigree Labrador who rejoices in the name of 'Wedgie'.

Hobbies

Golf; water sports; pipe-smoking. Colleagues tell me that I am a gifted raconteur.

Religious convictions if any

If Jesus Christ had wished women to be priests he would have chosen a woman as one of his apostles.

Ditto blacks, Americans, left-wingers of all complexions, people with moustaches, enthusiasts, Jews, et cetera, et cetera.

Favourite book

Anything by Jeffrey Archer or John Mortimer, both of whom I know personally.

If you had three wishes what would they be

I'm sorry but I'm a busy man, living in the real world.

What would you most like to be remembered for

My not unsmall hand in almost guiding through a Private Member's Bill calling for the abolition of obligatory tipping in restaurants.

Pet hate

The snobbery of the far left. All who destroy when they should be building.

Favourite catchphrase

Good question.

Are you frightened of death and if so why

With the greatest respect, this is the sort of carping, small-minded question I have grown used to over the years — and it always comes from a certain element, politically motivated, needless to say.

INTRODUCTION

by the Rt Hon. Norman Tebbit MP

Chairman of the Conservative Party

The vile misrepresentations and half-baked truths told by the pygmies, dwarves and other thoroughly small people financed wholly or in part by the top cats in the Kremlin that led to the tragic resignation in 1981 of Sir Shortley de Peverill, one of our most able post-war Junior Defence Ministers, have now been buried in the mists of time, and rightly so. I know that all my colleagues join me in welcoming this exceptionally able man back into the mainstream Conservative fold with the publication of these well-chosen words on How to Appeal to the Electorate.

Following his tragic resignation, Sir Shortley and his devoted wife Melissa refused to 'lie low', instead throwing themselves wholeheartedly into charity fundraising. Within less than a year they had climbed back from near bankruptcy to a position in which they have been able to afford an attractive stately home in the Southwest and a string of flats in London; their tragic children, too, have been seen to. Now Sir Shortley and his devoted wife Melissa are regularly seen together in public, and spend as much time together in private as proximity will allow.

I for one know how well-qualified is Sir Shortley to pen this advice for Conservative candidates. This is a man who has been through it all. Six times turned down by selection committees. Five elections lost. His once-safe seat won twice with massively decreased majorities. Three near-financial-scandals in eighteen months. And then the gruelling events that led to his tragic resignation in 1981. Cut and thrust. Rough and tumble. Slap and tickle. Here is a man who can give as good as he gets.

There is, as Sir Shortley makes clear, nothing in the slightest bit wrong with Conservative policies. Far from it. After many years of Conservative government, our police force has never been better armed. There are now fewer people than ever in our hospitals. Our armed forces are now backed by an impressive range of nuclear weaponry. And, as everyone knows, British Telecom has been privatised. Considerable achievements all. As Sir Shortley emphasises, our main concern as Conservatives should now be presentation. This is essential if we are to get ordinary men and women up and down the country believing that we care for them.

Finally, a word of praise for Sir Shortley Peverill's devoted wife Melissa, who has stood by him through thick and thin with her dignity intact. Many have compared her to a trooper, and I think the analogy holds true to this day.

NORMAN TEBBIT MP
Chairman of the Conservative
Party

'Caring for One, Caring for All'

by Sir Shortley de Peverill

Hello. Lovely to be with you again. And hello to you too.

From the heading above, you will gather that the Conservative slogan at the next election is, and I quote, 'Caring for One, Caring for All'. I think you will agree that this suggests a softer, more compassionate party than we put over in our tougher, perhaps more realistic slogans of 1979 ('Don't Come Running to Us'), 1983 ('Stop Whining'), and 1987 ('You've Only Yourself to Blame'). It is designed to show that the opposition parties have no monopoly on compassion.

Times have changed and we as Conservatives must change with them. I achieved my first election victory in 1978 with a no-holds-barred approach. My platform included the following personal pledges:

- I will not spend my time hanging around street corners in my constituency soliciting the problems and grievances of malcontents and ne'er-do-wells.
- The last thing I want is a house in this constituency.
- Capital punishment for train-fare dodgers.
- An end to obligatory tipping in restaurants.
- I will use my position as your Member of Parliament to further my own business interests.

I was successfully returned with a vastly decreased majority, but I've never placed much confidence in statistics. Nevertheless, the new Conservative approach is less forthright. We must now shake the hand we would once have handcuffed.

How to be selected as a Prospective Conservative Candidate

There was a time, just ten short years ago, when the following physical attributes guaranteed one a safe seat:

- an excess of nasal hair
- a decent brand of porridge nestling in one's moustache
- less than 200 hairs on crown of head
- a brace of pheasant strung around neck
- a regimental or Old Etonian tie strung around waist

But these have now been purged by all but the most far-flung constituency associations. In their place have come:
- gold buckles on shoes
- gold identity bracelet
- coat-hanger in back of car
- shaved palms
- 'casual-wear' drip-dri flared track suit

Let's take a closer look at the 'nu-style' candidate.

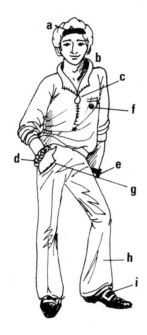

At this juncture, I must offer thanks to Mr Cecil Parkinson, Chairman of the Conservative Association for Disgraced Former Ministers, both for agreeing to pose for the above diagram and for his invaluable help and advice on Personal Appearance. A man of exceptional ability and a great communicator.

a A full head of hair spells drive. If, like Cecil, you secrete natural oil, your parting will retain its richness. Older and less hirsute or oil-rich members – I am thinking now of Lord Whitelaw – favour the invisible hairnet. A hair out of place could cost us this vital election.

b A track suit spells love of life. Wide lapels on a track suit spell breadth of compassion.

c A full breast pocket spells efficiency. Cecil is here seen carrying his portable electric toothbrush, his nasal hair tweezer, his nail varnish and his solid gold Rite-as-U-like biro-style Parker pen.

d Digital quartz gold Swiss British-made watch with full underwater facilities. 'I call it my wristwatch,' quips Cecil, 'because it's a watch – and it fits on my wrist!!'

e A gold identity bracelet inscribed 'For Cecil from your long-suffering but dignified wife Ann'. Touching.

f Eezi-so identity patch with initials 'CP'.

g Cecil favours the zip. 'I'm the sort of fellow who wears nothing underneath – and the housewives seem to like it that way!!' quips Cecil. This sort of attention to detail might make all the difference come polling day.

h Flared trousers spell 'young at heart'. 'That's me!' quips Cecil. 'I'm a great believer in the young and we must channel their idealism into Conservative votes. I have a lot of pop music and consider Andrew Lloyd Webber a genius – and an astute businessman to boot.'

i Gold buckled shoes are a vital part of modern Conservative thinking. Shoes tell you a lot about a man. 'My own are highly polished, artificial, comfortable and easily undone,' explains Cecil.

What to Believe

Now that you have kitted yourself out, it is as well to approach the local selection committee with a number of your beliefs already worked out. Practise beforehand on this questionnaire and you will learn to avoid the obvious pitfalls.

Gone are the days when it was safest to believe in capital punishment and blood sports alone: one must now have opinions about such apparently cloud-cuckoo subjects as the economy (money, etc.), social services (bus passes, etc.) and even foreign policy (things happening abroad).

QUESTIONNAIRE FOR CONSERVATIVE PARTY SELECTION COMMITTEES

1. Where do you stand on Capital Punishment?
   a) 'It never did me any harm.'   *10 points*
   b) 'Only if it's done tastefully.'   *8 points*
   c) 'I'm right behind Mrs Thatcher on this one.'   *20 points*
   d) 'Only if the fellow's guilty.'   *0 points*
   e) 'It's the ultimate detergent.'   *0 points*

2. What is your solution to the Northern Ireland problem?
   a) 'We must steer a steady course.'   *6 points*
   b) 'It is, of course, a deeply divided province.'   *6 points*
   c) 'I'm right behind Mrs Thatcher on this one.'   *20 points*
   d) 'We must shoot to kill the men of violence.'   *15 points*
   e) 'It won't go away.'   *18 points*

3. Is higher unemployment inevitable?
   a) 'I have personally heard of a man in the North drawing the dole while running his own chain of luxury hotels. Makes you think.'   *15 points*
   b) 'I'm right behind Mrs Thatcher on this one.'   *20 points*
   c) 'It is a fact that since Mrs Thatcher came to power there is not one working man in this country who is unemployed.'   *18 points*
   d) 'I wouldn't call it enviable, no, but it won't go away.'   *2 points*
   e) 'If all the unemployed of this country got jobs, there would be no unemployment – it's a fact.'   *18 points*

4. How would you alter Conservative foreign policy?

a) 'I'm right behind Mrs Thatcher on this one.' *20 points*

b) 'We must steer a steady course.' *6 points*

c) 'We should get everyone around a table.' *15 points*

d) 'It is as well to remember that we are an island nation.' *15 points*

e) 'Pray, let us have two minutes silence for the valiant heroes of the Falklands.' *19 points*

5. What are your particular interests within the political process?

a) 'I firmly believe that Britain has a lot to contribute.' *15 points*

b) 'I firmly believe that murderers and rapists should not be allowed to get away with it any longer.' *12 points*

c) 'I firmly believe in trade unions, but not if they abuse their power to further their members' interests.' *13 points*

d) 'I firmly believe in a firm belief in firm beliefs – and we must be quite firm in this belief.' *16 points*

e) 'I'm firmly behind Mrs Thatcher on this one.' *20 points*

PERSONAL SECTION

6. How do you relax?

a) 'I like meeting new colleagues and entertaining associates.' *10 points*

b) 'I have a single whisky and watch *One Man and his Dog* on television before turning in for an early night.' *8 points*

c) 'I am an active participant in my local Neighbourhood Watch scheme.' *15 points*

d) 'I either take my wife out for a quiet meal at a local restaurant or commit adultery with my secretary, no, only joking!' *Minus 18 points*

e) 'I put as much drive and energy into my play as I put into work. At the moment, for instance, I'm building up a comprehensive library of micro-computer software to further the home education of my two young children, John, 6, and Mary, 4½, while at the same time devoting as much time as possible to constructing a play-pavilion for local mentally handicapped children and raising money by means of fun-runs for victims of trade-union closed-shop agreements. I am a member of the local Round Table through the offices of which I conduct a Tidiness Campaign which within the space of one year has seen a 34 per cent drop in litter. In my position as Branch Secretary for the League of Cruel Sports I have doubled membership in two years. I enjoy yachting and playing golf with my wife Barbara and business friends and if ever I get a spare minute I screw my secretary, oh, damn, that's done it.' *Minus 20 points*

7. How would you involve yourself in the day-to-day life of the constituency?

a) 'Where are we now – somewhere in the North, isn't it?' *0 points*

b) 'Oh, I'd certainly drop by from time to time.' *3 points*

c) 'I would see to it that my wife and children would live here throughout the week, only joining me in London at weekends and during the recess.' *20 points*

d) 'I'm right behind Mrs Thatcher on this one.' *20 points*

e) 'If elected, I would buy a small Georgian mansion in the heart of the mining area; I would have my children educated here; I would open at least fifty church and local association fetes a year; I would conduct lengthy weekly surgeries; I would see to it that all my constituents, regardless of their politics, had their problems seen to; I would shop locally, appear on local TV and in the local press, support a number of local charity organisations, learn the full name and address of the constituency off by heart and set up a local love-nest with the wife of the constituency agent, oh, no, no, I wouldn't, no I'd do everything but that, oh, blast.' *Minus 20 points*

8. I'm afraid that this is rather personal, so I hope you'll forgive us, but do you have any area of – how should we put it – irregularity in your private or public life which we should be informed of before making our selection?

a) 'I love my wife and children, and I don't mind who knows it.' *18 points*

b) 'Only large-scale financial corruption – nothing worth reporting.' *18 points*

c) 'I fought for the Argies in the Falklands, but let's let bygones be bygones, shall we?' *Minus 20 points*

d) 'I have a long medical history of congenital fibbing.' *20 points*

e) 'I'll be frank. My wife is an alcoholic and sleeps around, often with other women. Both my children, Sandra, 16, and Harry, 25, are heroin addicts. My three illegitimate children, Ali, 14, Tariq, 13, and Ashram, 12, are all members of the League of Young Trotskyists and are avowed supporters of the policies of Colonel Qaddafi. I have three times been reported to the police by the Royal Society for the Prevention of Cruelty to Animals and I am an out-and-out homosexual of the first order. But I have sufficient confidence in you, your committee and the good people of this constituency, to know that you value truth above discretion and that you would never allow my personal plight to stand in the way of my undoubted abilities.' *Minus 50 points*

TURNING YOUR WIFE INTO AN ASSET

Me back again. Hello.

In my opinion, there are still three categories of person who constitute a very real electoral liability. These are:

a) *Our 'swarthy-complexioned' friends.*

If changes are to come about, they should be gradual.

b) *Females.*

With one most notable exception, the fairer sex – and no-one loves them more than I! – prove too anxious to get their own way when it comes to politics, and often, I find, they are far too ready to agree with the majority opinion. If changes are to come about, they should be gradual.

c) *Unmarried men.*

Suspicions will always linger, and the whiff of scandal can never be far away. A female wife lends dignity and colour to a politician – and proves most reassuring to the man in the street.

Choice of wife, must, I firmly believe, be left to the individual; nonetheless, it will behove him well to test his aspirant bride with the following constituency questionnaire:

QUESTIONS TO BE ASKED OF THE WIFE ALONE

1. What do you see as the main duties of the wife of an MP?
a) 'I see myself as primarily decorative.'   *20 points*
b) 'To stand by him when the press find out about it all.'   *20 points*
c) 'To involve myself at every level.'   *0 points*
d) 'I plan to enjoy myself as much as possible.'   *Minus 10 points*

2. What are your own broad political beliefs?
a) 'Sorry?'   *20 points*
b) 'I strongly believe that there should be more honest-to-goodness old-fashioned fun on television, particularly for our old folk in the afternoons. Whatever happened to entertainment, that's what I'd like to know.'   *18 points*
c) 'I'm right behind my husband on this one.'   *25 points*
d) 'Well, I disagree with my husband on one or two issues, for instance . . .'   *Minus 50 points*

APPEALING TO THE ELECTORATE

My career in politics began with a lengthy course at the University of Hard Knocks.

For those of you who have not heard this humorous expression before, it means that I had quite a tough time of it, but eventually learned from my mistakes. (I should make it clear at this point that I am in fact a proud graduate of the University of Oxford.)

Mistake Number One was to think I knew it all. I would make elementary factual errors in my speeches and television appearances and of course my opponents, politically motivated to a man, would leap on them to discredit me.

Here are just some of the elementary errors, reprinted here to save others my embarrassment:

A) *Common error:* Great Britain is a small island off Europe populated by a Royal Family and Joan Collins.

Fact: Great Britain is a major world power with incalculable influence in world affairs, particularly as regards the future of Cornwall.

B) *Common error:* The overwhelming majority of ordinary men and women up and down the country were educated at one of our major public schools.

Fact: Less than half the population were educated at public school. The rest went to 'state' schools, which admit girls.

C) *Common error:* The Falkland Islands are attached to the British mainland by a narrow isthmus, and are thus rightfully ours.

Fact: The Falkland Islands are not in fact attached to the British mainland, but are situated off the coast of South America. But the point holds.

D) *Common error:* 'Soon you will be saying that National Service should be abolished!'

Fact: National Service in Britain has in fact already been abolished, as long ago as 1961.

E) *Common error:* 'I've spoken to a hell of a lot of football hooligans, which I suspect is more than you have, and they all agree that they'd prefer to be given pills or the electric chair rather than have it hang over them for the rest of their born days.'

Fact: Many football hooligans enjoy being football hooligans.

Moral: Restrict your public speeches only to what you know. Thirty seconds speaking in public is a lot longer than you might think, and it is surprising how, after only twenty or so seconds, you will find yourself 'treading water' until the end. But speak longer, and you will undoubtedly be caught out by a Kremlin plant.

Mistake Number Two was to misjudge the generosity of the general public. In fact they are a pretty harsh lot, bigoted, ungrateful and often malicious.

I remember well when my son Shortley, then aged eighteen, good-humouredly raped an old-age pensioner of ninety-two after a night of high spirits on drugs and champagne. Sure enough, the great British public got on its customary high horse. Laughing it off with a quip along the lines of 'Natural high spirits for one of his tender years,' I was upbraided in the local press and abused in the streets. The British commodity of a good sense of humour is not one shared widely among our ever-increasing population, I fear.

The great unwashed had another of its periodic fits of moral outrage during the events that led to my tragic resignation in 1981. The details have been repeated endlessly in the gutter press and beyond. There is no need to repeat them here. It is now widely accepted that my then secretary, Miss de Sykes, became pregnant by me as part of a long-term offshore business development scheme that would have brought much hard-earned foreign currency into our beleaguered economy, and that there was nothing in any way 'underhand' or 'immoral' about my own part in the affair. That she is a pygmy, there is no doubt. That I am a man of honour is now beyond question.

Mistake Number Three was to see all publicity as good publicity. There was a time when I would send the local and national press any snippet of information about myself. This resulted in damaging headlines, including:

> **TORY RECEIVED CHILDREN THROUGH POST**
>
> **TORY EATS HAMSTER**
>
> **MP CALLS FOR MORE ORPHANS**
>
> **I SLEPT WITH MAGGIE CLAIMS BACKBENCHER**
>
> **QUEEN MOTHER 'COMMUNIST PLANT' CLAIMS MP**
>
> **MP CONDEMNS MOTHER TERESA**
>
> **BAN ALL BOOKS CALL FROM MP**

It soon became clear to me that not all publicity is good publicity.

WHEN THEY FIND OUT
FOR PRESENT MEMBERS OF PARLIAMENT ONLY

TICK whichever personal tragedy may apply to you:

ACTIVITY	REASON
☐ Alcoholism	Openness
☐ Bankruptcy	Charity work
☐ Prostitution (female)	Helping out close friend
☐ Prostitution (male)	Helping out pitiful wretch
☐ Impregnation of secretary	Betrayed by secretary
☐ Spying	Extending the hand of friendship
☐ Hand in till	Thought till belonged to me
☐ Child abuse	Thought he was dwarf
☐ Murder or attempted murder	Valuable defence work
☐ Bribery and corruption	Contributing to party funds

POSTSCRIPT: Making The Electorate See Sense

We in the rapidly-expanding Conservative Association of Disgraced Former Ministers have learned how to gain the trust of the General Public. It is this trust which will make all the difference come polling day.

What do I say on meeting a member of the General Public?
Always make a point of speaking to them as *individuals* on an equal footing with yourself. Vary your comment with the profession and appearance of the person you are addressing. They will love you for it. Thus: –

To a miner: *'Grubby work, eh? Good for you!'*
To a policeman: *'I should think you come across some rum types. Good for you!'*
To a trade-union official: *'I strongly believe in trade unions, but not if they wield power. Good for you!'*
To the unemployed: *'You're doing a marvellous job. Good for you!'*
To a black person: *'I can see that you wouldn't mug anyone. Good for you!'*
To a woman: *'Mustn't interrupt your washing. Good for you!'*
To your mistress: *'No baby today? Good for you!'*

Do remember that everyone you meet is an *individual* with fears and worries, hopes and ambitions all his own. He will wish to know what *you* are going to do for *him* and *his family* if elected – and he'll engage you in exacting argument if he doesn't think you've given him the right reply!
For this reason, I strongly recommend avoiding all individuals.
Alternatively, you should shake his hand and say, 'I only wish I had time to answer that very interesting point, but I can't spend all day talking to riff-raff when there's an election in the air. Good afternoon.'
He will respect your no-nonsense approach and remember you for it come polling day.

Thank you so much for allowing me into your home. I've so much enjoyed writing this for you. Remember, any problems, I'm so sorry to hear them!

Name

Lady Eva de Topliss

Date of birth

Profession

Party Organiser and Tireless Charity Worker.

Position currently held

President and Patron, The Golden Square Ball. Entertainments Secretary to the National Trust. Founder and Managing Director, Eva-So-Posh Parties Ltd.

Family

My husband Sir Bantock de Topliss is a great help with chairs, etc. My very dear children Sarah and the other one also make appearances at very special parties if they've behaved well.

Achievements to date

Betty Kenward ('Jennifer' of Jennifer's Diary) tells me that there is no one like me, that I have single-handedly brought fun and correct behaviour back into British parties, and that my tireless charity work on behalf of the over-privileged has earned me the (extra) title of Saint – but I'm sure she's just being kind, because she is an awfully kind little woman, whatever people might say.

Awards

My only award is to see other people enjoying themselves.

High point of career

I had the great honour of organising the fifth birthday party of Miss Zara Phillips, daughter of HRH Princess Anne and her husband. I have also had the tremendous privilege of organising many other Royal do's, notably Zara Phillips's third and fourth birthday parties, and also her second.

Low point of career

In 1985, the gutter press 'discovered' that my father Gunther von Topliss had been an avowed Nazi, and a member of Hitler's private staff. During the following harrowing weeks, I managed to discover that he had been no more than Chief Entertainments Officer, but the damage had been done, and may well affect the sales of my next book, *What Happens When You Die – And How to Rustle Up a Fondue*.

Best friend

I suppose my greatest failing is that I absolutely adore people, particularly people I haven't had the pleasure of meeting before. So in answer to your question, 'Who is your best friend?', I would have to reply, 'The very next person I meet!'

What makes you happy

I'm actually a very shy person, and very family-minded, so I like nothing more than to spend a – very occasional alas – quiet night in with my husband and family and two hundred or so close friends.

What makes you sad

Seeing my husband Sir Bantock de Topliss struggling with up to two thousand chairs he has kindly agreed to arrange in lines for a party, desperately trying to conceal the pain caused by his bad back from me. But I would never ask him to stop arranging chairs — it's his whole life these days.

What qualities do you look for in a human being

A sense of humour is vital. I don't like people with chips on their shoulders and I hate cynics. I disapprove strongly of people who flout convention — it's so conventional!! I hate bad manners. But a sense of humour is vital.

Most memorable disaster

Catering for four hundred, my devoted cook, a perfectionist, made enough soup for only three hundred and fifty and consequently committed voluntary suicide. But with the aid of water and a few stock cubes, no one noticed, thank goodness!

Heroes

Jesus Christ gave one of the most memorable dinner parties ever, so he must be a hero, though to be frank if I had been organising that wedding at Canaan I would have given the caterers a rocket.

Ambitions

I'm not ambitious for myself: I would be perfectly happy to live on a small island in Scotland with only my husband, our border terrier and a small marqueeful of reasonably titled people for company; but my workers would be *so* disappointed.

If you weren't yourself who would you choose to be

Mother Teresa of Calcutta: a caterer like myself, only *what* a caterer!

Pets if any

A border terrier called Spats; and all my lovely staff of course!

Hobbies

Flower arrangement; writing (one collection of poems, *A Garland of Doves*, has already been privately published); helping others with small acts of great kindness; studying people: a lifetime's course!

Religious convictions if any

I regard God as one of my very closest friends; I can tell Him anything: He's that sort of person. If ever I do something the teensiest bit naughty, I just have to apologise and He lets me off. A chum indeed. I also know a lot of people He knows, and His mother, the Virgin Mary, charming, absolutely charming, has been a dear friend of the family for literally yonks. They're both great fun, and, more importantly, *good with people*.

Favourite book

Mind Your Backs – Britain in the 1980s by HRH Prince Philip, a cousin of mine, contains much no-nonsense advice for politicians.

If you had three wishes what would they be

1. The perfect dinner party for six – HRH Prince Philip, Terence de Brittish, Countess Spencer, little Ronnie Corbett, Margaret Duchess of Argyll and myself: mmmmm!
2. A 'talent evening' with the Royals: Margaret on piano, Philip doing his duck calls, Queen Mum on dummy guitar, Fergie doing her 'blancmange' turn.
3. Dinner *à deux* with Harold Acton reading from his verse collection *Peonies and Ponies.*

What would you most like to be remembered for

The many small acts of kindness I have performed for others better off than myself; leaving the world a happier, jollier place than it was when I found it. If that's a snobbish wish then I'm sorry, but I must confess to being a snob!

Pet hate

People who talk about our country in terms of class – so old-fashioned. I've had Lorraine Chase *and* Norman Tebbit at my parties (and, I may say, they both behaved beautifully).

Favourite catchphrase

What is a 'catchphrase'?

Are you frightened of death and if so why

Far too busy.

COME AS A FRIEND – LEAVE AS A STRANGER

LADY EVA DE TOPLISS'S GUIDE TO SUCCESSFUL PARTY-GIVING

☆ *Why am I throwing this party?*

Parties can be divided into four neat groups. Identifying the category your party slips into means half the battle won.

1. To make money.

This type of party is becoming increasingly popular, particularly with the young. Rather than waste a fortune pouring good money down people's throats, many go-ahead young people (I've always had a great regard for the young) have hit upon the bright idea of charging their 'friends' for the variety of services they provide. And a jolly good thing too.

One small caveat. Though quite willing to pay 'through the nose' for meeting new friends in grand surroundings, many partygoers prefer to settle up after, rather than during, the celebration. My advice:

DON'T employ a turnstile in between reception area and dance floor. INSTEAD: extract cash (no credit cards – awful bother) as your guests get out of their cars or vehicles.

DON'T charge for the first drink of the evening: guests like to be made to feel at home. INSTEAD: charge them per bottle consumed or portion thereof – this will include the first drink, but will not cause undue offence.

DON'T spend an arm and a leg hiring a fly-by-night

celebrity. INSTEAD: Remember that the drawing power of even a minor Royal like my friend Marie-Christine – HRH Princess Michael of Kent to you – is such that the small expense involved in a well-chosen presentation gift (I always advise a Jaguar and/or a new gardener) is as nothing when compared to the financial goodwill they can generate.

2. To get something out of someone.

Perhaps you are contemplating a divorce and wish to demonstrate your spouse's wealth to on-site solicitors. Perhaps you are planning a celebration in honour of an elderly friend or friends who might be planning to leave you 'a little something' in their will or wills. Perhaps you wish to put nouveau next-door neighbours firmly in their place by requesting their services as hired helps for the night. You'll find there's always a good enough reason for a party!

3. To successfully launch a product or products.

There's nothing quite like a ballroomful of friends and business associates (and what's the difference these days?) gathered together to celebrate the arrival of a new consumer-oriented product as part of an overall marketing strategy.

The days are happily long gone since it was considered somehow 'not quite right' to talk of business at a party. In a free country (and remember ours still *is* a free country, despite what some might say) business is the glue that binds society, and as such is not to be sniffed at.

A new product is a godsend to an imaginative Party Organiser like myself, but when I was asked by the managing director of an internationally renowned company to come up with a theme party based around a new reusable plastic toothpick I readily admit that for a few seconds even I was baffled.

Be Bold. I straightaway ordered 10,000 of the company's reusable toothpicks.

3000 of them I set aside for a little man I know who can

work wonders with anything. Within the space of twenty-four hours he had transformed the toothpicks into a life-size model of HRH Princess Michael of Kent who had graciously agreed to be present in person on the evening itself.

Another firm with which I am associated ran me up a gigantic set of teeth, six feet high when fully open.

I then suspended Princess Michael from the ceiling with transparent strings, pointing head first into the huge teeth. All it now needed was 'gunge' – I improvised with a discarded wedding cake – to be inserted in the teeth and the illusion was complete. Of course, Marie-Christine's sharp features are ideally suited for use as a toothpick – another example of my extraordinary good luck!

Marie-Christine was simply thrilled upon seeing this imaginative exhibit. 'That's the first time I've been called a toothpick!' she quipped, and we all had a good laugh. She is a great sport, and has a highly developed sense of her own ridiculousness – a very necessary quality for someone in her position! She later wrote a charming letter thanking me for the new kitchenmaid.

I asked a Leading Fashion House to transform the remaining *7000* toothpicks into a dazzling ball-gown with full train and tiara. It was quite the most dashing costume I have ever worn. Uncomfortable? A little, but to ensure the success of a party one must always make sacrifices.

I may say I timed my entrance perfectly. I had ensured that the assembled collection of party-goers (many of them in the toothpick game themselves, or representatives from the toothpick trade press) had been well fed on my teeth-clogging cerise and vermilion Gooey Oatcake Specials.

A well-placed assistant judged when the party-goers' teeth were at their most clogged – some of the less well educated had already begun to thrust their fingers into their mouths, rootling around in the most ungainly fashion – and, bang on time, gave me the rehearsed signal to enter.

'Gentlemen,' I announced, 'the reusable plastic tooth-picks are on me!' and with that there was a visible rush. Toothpicks were stripped from my person at the rate of knots. Soon everyone in the ballroom was picking away, and I was left standing in a maroon and apricot under-garment I had specially selected for the occasion. As might have been expected, the managing director of the company, quite thrilled, went on exploring my body for hidden toothpicks, but that's another story.

4. To further one's social standing.

I am told that it has become fashionable in left-wing circles to knock those ordinary folk who wish, through sheer hard grind, to reach a position in our society from which they can look down on others.

This snobbish attitude has nothing to do with the old socialism on which I was brought up. In those days, socialism meant just that – being social, and if this involved throwing a glamorous ball, well, so much the better!

I think it was George Orwell who said that communism might work in theory but never in practice. True words indeed! Take parties. There must be a little woman looking after the coats and a man in charge of clearing up the lavatories ('toilets' (!)), just as there must also be a host and hostess. The little woman and the little man would be perfectly miserable if they were forced to become host and hostess for the evening, and anyway they couldn't possibly afford it.

Everyone should wish to further his – or her – social standing. I have even seen Her Majesty the Queen, incidentally married to a cousin of mine, showing school-girlish excitement at the prospect of meeting Mr Bob Monkhouse, and who can honestly blame her? Now, when she visits one of our further flung Central African outposts, it gives her an extra special thrill to tell Their Straw-skirted Heads of State that she has personally met the presenter of *Bob's Full House*. It's a great ice-breaker, and I daresay many marvellous new trade deals and inter-cultural exchanges could not have been possible without Her Majesty's wide range of show-biz anecdotes.

I am often asked to procure members of the Aristocracy to add 'tone' to a social gathering of those who, though wealthy, through no fault of their own are not yet titled. Frankly, this costs quite a bit, and should not be attempted by those working to a limited budget. How well I remember one memorable occasion when I was asked at the very last

HRH QUEEN ELIZABETH II
Official Smile 'n' Frown Graph

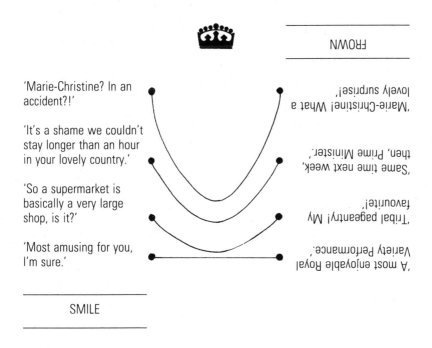

FROWN

'Marie-Christine? In an accident?!'

'Marie-Christine! What a lovely surprise!'

'It's a shame we couldn't stay longer than an hour in your lovely country.'

'Same time next week, then, Prime Minister.'

'So a supermarket is basically a very large shop, is it?'

'Tribal pageantry! My favourite!'

'Most amusing for you, I'm sure.'

'A most enjoyable Royal Variety Performance.'

SMILE

moment to find ten Countesses who were prepared, at the drop of a hat, to fly to the Bournemouth Conference Centre and model outsize swimwear to a gathering of international leisurewear manufacturers. Though one or two required some assurance that the dignity of their position would not be impaired by such a display, I managed to rally the full quota within the half hour. I was even informed later that Bubbles, Countess Rothermere, a very dear friend of mine, was most disappointed not to have been asked herself, but I soon grasped the opportunity to unruffle her feathers when asked later the same week to organise an event for a company specialising in hot-air balloons. The sight of Bubbles floating high in the air powered only by a huge bunsen burner is one that will stay with me for many years.

One comes across it so often: the social climber who extends an invitation to one with the express intention of being invited back. In these circumstances, it is much better to be kind to be cruel. Accept their invitation, enjoy yourself as much as poss. and include this postscript in your thank-you letter:

'P.S.
We are having a few old and very dear friends around for cocktails next Tuesday. We would love to have invited you too, but feel that you would not feel "comfortable" – they tend to be very "correct"! But we enclose "a little something" to put towards a bottle of sherry or cheap wine of your choice, for home consumption only. Much more cosy!'

But remember – every man, woman and child on this planet can be put to good use. Even the most tongue-tied wallflower can lend a hand handing around the 'eats': she should then be drawn into the conversation with friendly, 'ad lib' remarks. These are three that work a treat:
– 'Celia never says a thing, do you, dear?'
– 'She's nothing to look at, but give her a plate and she'll pass it around beautifully, ha ha!'
– 'Did anyone see that marvellous film, *The Helen Keller Story*?'

Parties given for christenings, weddings, anniversaries or funerals can be neatly fitted into any one of the above categories. How well I remember a highly successful launch for a new line of disposable babywear at the christening of my eldest niece. I 'doubled up' the funeral of my dear old grandmother – a remarkable lady and a very close confidante – with a drinks party to pay back a number of (rather dull) people who lived locally.

Nowadays it is quite the 'done thing' to charge wedding guests a small consideration on everything from the parking space provided for their car or cars to the slice of wedding cake they have come to expect: all these things cost money and there is no reason at all why it should be *you* who has to 'carry the can'. From the profits of my second marriage I financed the most marvellous skiing holiday in Verbier: a winter break to cherish for the rest of my life.

There are still, I believe, a small number of people who insist on throwing parties for 'fun'. I always advise clients against falling into this trap. There is nothing remotely 'fun' about watching other people drink you out of house and home. Even your closest friends or spouse will not be above finding their fingers straying in the direction of that irreplaceable silver teaspoon or that candelabrum you picked up for next to nothing on your maiden aunt's deathbed. 'Fun' is a word too often heard employed by drug addicts and hooligans in the courtrooms for it to cut any ice with me.

Very Dear Friends

May I be honest with you for a minute?

I have excluded one category of party simply because I assume that if you're the type of person who needs to buy a book such as this, then, frankly, you're not the sort who's going to have much opportunity to socialise with our Royal Family.

But Her Majesty the Queen has granted me her gracious permission to grant those of you on the other side of the social barrier a 'peek through the ramparts' as it were.

So here it is – a once-in-a-lifetime opportunity to escape from the little world that encloses you into the larger-than-life world of the Royal Family as they set about enjoying a right royal barbecue!

Like any British family, each Royal has his own very special role to play in the traditional 'fry-up' on the wild and windy moors near Balmoral.

The Duke of Edinburgh spends his country mornings watching birds and then, as his stomach-rumbles begin to signal that magic word 'lunch', he sets about shooting them. Not for him the palaver of periwigged footmen, attendant butler, chefs and valets, keepers and beaters: he stands alone on the moor, peppering the landscape with shot from his family 12-bore.

The Duke then grills his 'bag' on a barbecue he designed himself. Here's one of his typical menus – fit for a real-life Queen!

MENU

Gin from the Bottle

Smoked Woodlouse on Toast

Heinz Cream of Tomato Soup 'from the can'

Dead Grouse cooked in its feathers

Mixed Grill: Bacon (2 rashers), Egg, Tomato, Robin

Gin from the Bottle

An air of informality rules: speeches are kept to a minimum and medals are optional.

The Queen Mother believes that a good strong gale can blow all germs away. 'Couldn't we find somewhere a little more windy?' she is prone to suggest when a picnic site is chosen. Resplendent in waders and sou'wester, she can often be spotted taking *her* lunch up to her waist in a fast-flowing loch.

Eighty-seven-years-young, the nation's favourite great-granny loves nothing more than a round of poker and a bottle of port with her beloved grandchildren after a full morning's eating. 'You owe me a tenner. I'll give you till noon tomorrow, small fry,' she has been heard to quip to Prince Harry – and little Harry knows that no-nonsense Gran means business!

The Duke and Duchess of York enter into the spirit of things by taking charge of the Party Games – and the right royal funsters know how to enjoy themselves, that's for sure! A game of rounders followed by 'Kick the Can' and then a quick spin at fellatio is their idea of a hilarious afternoon – and, if there's still time before tea, a swift circle of Pass-the-Parcel finished off with some discipline lessons from leather-clad Fergie!

The Prince and Princess of Wales love to throw their Royal duties to the wind and relax in the wilds of Scotland, much as any other young lovebirds with kiddies. Away from the constant glare of press and TV cameras, they can let their hair down. 'Have you been waiting here long?' asks the Prince of his grandmother, while the Princess asks her barbecuing father-in-law, 'How long have you been working here?' Meanwhile, young Prince William practises waving at any wildlife he spots.

Prince Edward, keen to live down his 'limp-wristed' press image, reads his copy of *June and Schoolfriend* standing bare-chested in the pouring rain. A brilliant young actor and natural mimic, he has the whole family in stitches with his impersonation of Mary Poppins. 'But it's meant to be Rambo,' he explains.

HRH The Queen cherishes every minute of her Balmoral barbecues: it is on the Highland moors where she can for once be herself, and she takes to 'ordinary life' like a duck to water! Away from the pomp and pageantry of state occasions, she can return to what she likes doing best – the washing-up.

Even before lunch is finished, Her Majesty slips off into her 'little hut' – an exact replica of Sandringham, but without a dishwasher – switches on Radio 2 and whistles while she washes.

WARNING: It is advisable to keep an eye on Her Majesty while she is doing the washing-up. In her busy life, she has found little time to become expert at the activity, and some observers have reported finding her with rubber gloves on her head, throwing out the plates and scrubbing the leftovers clean.

Once you have pinpointed what type of party you wish to throw, then half the battle is won!

Next, check that you have the following things, each of them *essential* to the success of any party:

Drink
I always recommend a highly-coloured 'punch' as a splendid way of getting rid of all those kitchen leftovers. Here is my secret recipe – never known to fail!

1 bottle Curacao	*1 bucket Potato Peel*
1 bottle Sparkling White Wine	*1 bottle Brandy* or *Armagnac*
(preferably Méthode	*2 bottles Medium-Dry Cyder*
Champagnoise)	*4 Bacon Rinds*
½ lb Giblets	*1 carton Sour Cream*
1 bottle Port	*½ cup of Bisto*

Cutlery
Each of your guests will expect to be given, on loan of course, his own knife and fork.

I always think that table settings are terribly important, and I have never gone along with the current practice of 'not bothering' to lay a table correctly.

Conversation
It is fatal to try to predict or control the flow of conversation. Nevertheless, I have found in my 25-odd years of party organising that guests *do* appreciate certain guidelines upon which to base their talk. If you fail to follow these simple guidelines, you may well find that your conversation runs out well before the end of your party!

BASIC FOUR-COURSE PLACE SETTING

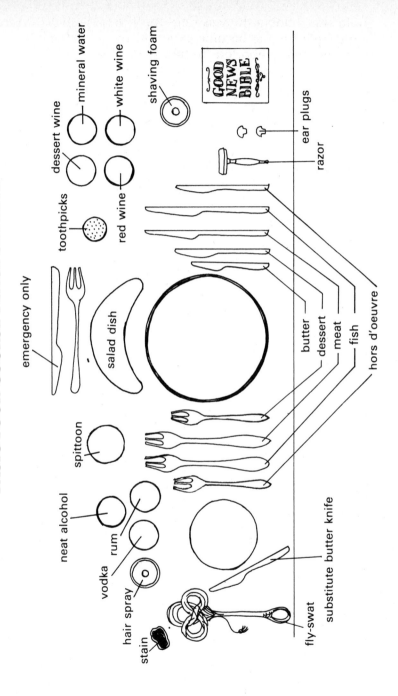

- dessert wine
- mineral water
- white wine
- red wine
- toothpicks
- shaving foam
- GOOD NEWS BIBLE
- ear plugs
- razor
- emergency only
- salad dish
- butter
- dessert
- meat
- fish
- hors d'oeuvre
- spittoon
- neat alcohol
- vodka
- rum
- hair spray
- stain
- fly-swat
- substitute butter knife

Upon Entry
Shall I take your coats?
Brrr! Ah, that's better!
Can I get you a drink?

Once In
What route did you take?
How are the children?
Top-up?
I got them from Peter Jones but I think they're worth it.
Top-up?
Sorry, what route did you say you took?

In the Dining Room
No, you're there, that's right, and you are there, good, no, not
 there . . .
Mmmmm, lovely.
How did you make it or is it top secret, ha ha.
Oh, you could have knocked ten minutes off by taking the A3054,
 I always say.
Oh, just a little. Lovely.

Second Course
Mmmmm, lovely smell.
Doesn't that look delicious!
How are the children?
Just a little. Lovely.
I *think* I'm a Gemini. I can never remember!
It's not just Rock Hudson.
I really can't see how Arthur Scargill comes into it.

Dessert
Bang goes my diet!
No, just a little. It looks lovely.
I find that new intersection awfully muddling.
I wouldn't have her job for the world!
How are the children?
Leave you to it!

After Dinner

MEN	WOMEN
Hold the country to ransom.	Portugal this year.
Just a drop.	How are the children?
The vast majority.	I find it stops me sleeping.
Just a drop. Thanks. Mmmm.	Scorpio? Of course!

Men	Women
Lot of respect . . .	Do let's see them!
Ordinary men and women . . .	Which one's that?
Just a drop. I'm driving.	We thought of Scotland.
Agree to differ, ha ha!	Difficult stage . . .

On Leaving
I'd take the A3054 if I were you.
Absolutely lovely.
How are the children?
Brrr! Chilly!
Controlled inflation.
Expansion inevitable.
Thank you so much!
Because it's quite obvious you've had too . . .
Byeee!
Let's not argue now.
Byee! Byee! Byee!

Afterwards
Certainly drank enough.
Let's leave it till the morning.
It's not *him* I mind.
Who's interested in her bloody children?
Who could have told them about it?
Bound to lose their way.
Left her coat.
I'll switch them off . . .

Food
Why not try something just that little bit different to liven up your next dinner party?

'Food Alive!' was the title I gave to my exciting 3-day cookery course last summer, and it was so successful that I'm already taking bookings for next year!

Like all good things, it's based on a very simple idea. For a long time, I've felt that the traditional three-course meal, e.g.:

THREE-COURSE MEAL
First Course
Second Course
Third Course

has become rather too predictable. Of course, some –
mainly foreign – chefs have tried to liven it up a bit, e.g.:

THREE-COURSE MEAL
First Course
Third Course
Second Course

but after a while the novelty wears rather thin.

My 'Food Alive!' programme sought to change all this. I
had noticed that, over the years, my dinner guests had
grown less and less interested in discussing what one might
call the 'current topics of the day' – the return of the death
penalty, the need for safety belts, the Channel Tunnel,
corporal punishment and so on and so forth – and were
increasingly interested in talking about the food itself, and
particularly the raw materials that had gone into each
recipe.

I sensed that, if one was serving them, say, chicken, they
would very much like to be able to actually see the chick-
chick-chicken clucking around on the table before eating
their fill of him (or her!).

With this in mind, I converted the smaller sitting room
into an aviary-cum-bestiary, which meant removing the
television to the drawing room, but one can't have
everything. The scheme proved an immediate hit with one
and all. Let's now take a look at how it works in practice:

The 'Food Alive' Three-Course Meal

1) First Course Preview
A live pheasant, a shotgun and a Moulinex are brought to the
table. As the pheasant wanders around the table and flies about
the room, the following conversation is suggested:

    GUEST A: 'Isn't that a pheasant?'
    GUEST B: 'Mmmm! Delicious!'

When this conversation has run its course, my dear husband
picks up the shotgun and peppers the bird, taking care to avoid
guests.

GUEST C: 'Good shot sir!'

I then pop the dead or dying bird into the Moulinex, feathers and all, flick the switch and – hey presto! – in 45 seconds my guests are eating their

2) First Course: Pheasant Soup
   GUEST A: 'Isn't this pheasant soup?'
   GUEST B: 'Mmmm! Delicious!'

3) Second Course Preview
A young spring lamb, dressed in a pretty pink ribbon, is then paraded around the room, skipping and gambolling in the candlelight.
   GUEST A: 'Isn't that a young spring lamb?'
   GUEST B: 'Mmmm! Delicious!'

My dear husband then erects a noose on the beam to the left of the dining table, and in a jiffy the lamb is swinging from it. DO remember to save the pink ribbon, though. With a good sharp knife, cut off a segment that will fit easily into the Moulinex, flick the switch and – hey presto! – in two minutes your guests are eating their:

4) Second Course: Casserole of Raw Young Spring Lamb
   GUEST A: 'Isn't this a raw young spring lamb?'
   GUEST B: 'Mmmm! Delicious!'

5) Third Course Preview
A cow is brought in.
   GUEST A: 'Isn't that a cow?'
   GUEST B: 'Mmmm! Delicious!'

My dear husband then milks the cow.
   ME: 'There'll now be a short wait as we wait for it to turn to yoghurt.'

☆ *How to Deal with Things That Go Wrong*

No party is entirely trouble-free. As a general rule, it is best to imagine that anything that *can* go wrong, *will* go wrong.

I end with a short checklist of the most common problems I have encountered at parties, and the means I have developed over the years to cope with them:

Drug Addicts
The titled folk I welcome to my own parties tend to bring their own supplies. Nevertheless, it is only polite to hire a state-registered nurse for the evening. Some party-givers swear by hiring a professional 'pusher', but this is only strictly necessary when entertaining anyone above the rank of Life Peer.

Suicides
Every good party has its fair number of suicides, but there is no reason why they should ruin it for others. If a guest chooses to kill himself while everyone else is managing to enjoy themselves, then that is entirely his own affair.

I find the best way of dealing with the corpse is to put it in a spare fridge. If it is still kicking, the extra cold should do the trick.

Heart Attacks on the Dance Floor
With so many senior guests these days only too willing to take to the dance floor for any up-tempo number, it is scarcely surprising that there are heart attacks galore at any successful party.

Rather than stop the music and ruin the party atmosphere, I have found that much the best thing is to 'laugh it off', reassuring guests by pretending it's all part of the fun!

Smuggle the corpse out by inserting it into a Conga line at the end of the party.

And, finally, that perennial problem:–

☆ *Getting Rid of Stragglers*

With both arms outstretched in a gesture of greeting, shout, at the top of your voice, 'Raine! At last!'

Lady Eva de Topliss's
A–Z of Party Chatter

A **A little present.** A very little present.
B **Bring a bottle.** . . . and get half a papercup full.
C **Can I get you a drink?** Can I stop dancing with you?
D **Don't bother to dress up.** Black tie.
E **Energetic.** Noisy.
F **Fun.** Balloons on display.
G **Great fun.** Lager available.
H **Huge fun.** Someone was sick.
I **I think I love you.** I think I'm drunk.
J **Just a few friends in.** No one we really wanted.
K **Knitted by you?** Hope you didn't pay money for it!
L **Let's talk about you now.** Let's carry on talking about me.
M **Mwah!** Noise made when enemies kiss.
N **Never mind.** I'll send you the cleaning bill.
O **On the subject of Aids** . . . 1.30 in the morning.
P **Pleased to meet you.** More pleased still to get away from you.
Q **Quiz game.** Time to leave.
R **Russian imperialism.** 2.30 in the morning.
S **See you soon.** Unless you duck first.
T **Treasure.** Old or foreign worker on 1950s wages.
U **Ulster question.** 3.30 in morning.
V **Very well thank you.** Migraine, bad back, divorce impending.
W **Will Nescafé do?** Nescafé will do.
X **Xmas cheer.** Couple of party hats and Cilla on TV.
Y **You shouldn't have.** You should have.
Z **ZZZZZZZzzzzzzz.** The company sparkled.

Name

Stewart R. de Stuart

Date of birth

January 23rd, 1922

Profession

Broadcasting Executive

Position currently held

Head of Fresh Ideas, BBC Television

Family

Currently married to Priscilla Rantzen, sister of TV's famous Esther. Two sons, Stewart, 30, and R., 26.

Achievements to date

Head of Internal Memoranda, BBC Television, 1952–56; Head of External Catering, BBC Television, 1956–61; Head of International Broadcasting (Recruitment), BBC Television, 1961–63; Head of Light Entertainment (Accounts), BBC Television, 1963–69; Director of Supervisory Data (Experimental Drama), BBC Television, 1969–73; Executive Controller, Documentary Features, BBC Television, 1973–80; Head of Fresh Ideas, BBC Television, 1980–87.

Awards

Order of the British Empire, 1975.

High point of career

Must surely be my presentation to Her Majesty Queen Elizabeth The Queen Mother on the occasion of my visit to the location of BBC TV's award-winning documentary series *Happy and Glorious* in 1977. 'Stuart,' she said radiantly. 'That sounds to me like a Scottish name.' 'That is correct, ma'am,' I replied. A proud moment indeed.

Low point of career

None so far!

Best friend

None so far! I have enjoyed good working relationships with all my colleagues in the Corporation over the years and this has made my tasks all the easier.

What makes you happy

Any programme with Terry Scott and June Whitfield.
A well-made documentary feature.
A joke by Barry Norman.
Keeping within budget.

What makes you sad

People who don't realise the value for money offered by the BBC.
A natural disaster in Country A – when our camera crew is in
Country B!
Needless waste.
A mournful ballad sung by the King's Singers.

What qualities do you look for in a human being

Lack of bias.

Most memorable disaster

I'd prefer to concentrate on the Corporation's achievements.

Heroes

The New Christy Minstrels.

Ambitions

To continue my career at the BBC to the best of my abilities.

If you weren't yourself who would you choose to be

I have great respect for Michael Grade.
I think that David Attenborough brings great professionalism to a fascinating career.

Pets if any

I enjoy all Wildlife programmes.

Hobbies

I enjoy watching Natural History programmes and also any programmes which broaden our knowledge of the world around us. I have a great sense of humour, so I always enjoy light comedy, but only if it is based in recognisable situations. I enjoy gardening and golf, especially on an excellent, large-size set.

Religious convictions if any

Regular viewer of the admirable *Songs of Praise*. Many long-playing albums by Harry Secombe.

Favourite book

I loved Charles Dickens's *David Copperfield* produced by Erskine Clarke jointly with ABC Television in 1975.

If you had three wishes what would they be

1. Full televised coverage of both Houses of Parliament.
2. An increase in the space allotted to Current Affairs in an enlarged *Radio Times*.
3. A television licence fee directly linked to the rate of inflation.

What would you most like to be remembered for

Television coverage of the wedding of HRH The Princess Anne and Captain Mark Phillips, October 1974.

Pet hate

People who don't pay their TV licence fees and yet enjoy all the facilities of television at the expense of others.

Favourite catchphrase

I don't have one of my own, but I get particular pleasure from hearing top TV conjuror Paul Daniels say, 'Not a lot, not a lot!'

Are you frightened of death and if so why

No – as long as it is treated with tact and good sense and does not cause unnecessary offence. I would advise a late-night slot, though.

Getting On in The BBC

by Stewart R. de Stuart OBE

Head of Fresh Ideas BBC-TV

Television is the most powerful medium in the history of mankind.

Tell me if I'm going too fast.

If the playwright William Shakespeare were alive today I would hazard a guess that he would be a lighting designer within the Beeb or similar. As an intelligent man, he would be drawn to the power of the medium and my friends who are still in conventional drama tell me that he enjoyed making full use of dramatic effects.

And we at the Beeb are always on the lookout for budding Shakespeares.

Perhaps you are the Shakespeare of make-up. In which case our make-up department would be delighted to hear from you.

Or are you the Shakespeare of special effects question mark. In which case our special effects department would be delighted to hear from you. Marshall Maclaverty called us a 'Global Village'. I seem to remember from my history lessons that Shakespeare lived in a theatre named the Globe, and those were the days before celebrities such as my good friend John Humphreys, the lads and lassies of *Tomorrow's World* et al.

If you want to get on in the BBC you could do worse than to follow my advice in the pages that follow. I'm not saying you'll end up as a Shakespeare or a Michael Grade, but it's a deeply satisfying career prospect.

What is a Fresh Idea question mark

Let's look at some of the freshest, brightest ideas that have been batted around the BBC in the past few years. It might also give you some indication of the high quality programming that will be on your screens throughout the next two decades.

A Light-Hearted Look at Car Maintenance with Dave Lee Travis.

A Seventh Series of *Jim'll Fix It* with your host Jimmy Savile OBE.

Tring Tring: A colourful history of the telephone presented by Professor Laurie Taylor.

The British Heritage: A lavish fifteen-part prestige series, with Sir Alfred Weedon OBE conducting us on a tour of our magnificent British Heritage.

Saturday Arts Programme: An innovative arts programme which takes a fresh look at what's happening each week in the world of arts with Denis Norden and Clive James.

Wildlife Special — The Robin: What makes the garden robin tick?

Going! Going! Gone!: Fun for all the family with a new TV comedy series with Paul Eddington as an auctioneer who gets more trouble than he bids!

Sunny Sunday!: In this lively new series from our Religious Affairs unit, David Essex, Robin Nedwell, Faith Brown and Dorothy Squires explain what being a Christian really means to them.

Easy as Winking: Can you wink faster than our team of celebrities? Pit your lids against Esther Rantzen, Lady Eva de Topliss, Richard Briers and Pamela Armstrong.

Hamlet: More riotous goings-on in a small Cotswolds village.

Different from Us?: Paul Heiney visits a tribe of natives in Brazil and asks the question 'Are they really all that different from us?'

Speak Your Mind: Viewers get a chance to put their views across on an issue of the day (Southwest only).

Andre Previn Plays: Peter Allis enjoys a round of golf with Andre Previn.

Stendhal — His Life and Work: More japes with Ricky Stendhal in his madcap aviary.

Around the Corner: Our team go out on the street and find some pretty surprising things are happening there.

Cause for Concern: New series in which Esther Rantzen takes a sideways look at heart disease and asks some important questions.

A Right Sew-and-Sew: The light-hearted way to teach yourself to sew (afternoons).

Mastermind: A new series hosted as usual by Magnus Magnusson.

Llennlulli Llennlich (for viewers in Wales).

Darts from Bournemouth: Darts from Bournemouth.

As you can see for yourselves, the above list buries once and for all the current notion that the BBC is short of fresh ideas. The above list shows just what imaginative, lively programming can do.

You will find something for everyone and much to enjoy for yourself I feel sure.

May I say at this point that we are particularly proud to have secured the world rights to exclusive coverage of Darts at Bournemouth. This will be screened later in the year under the programme title *Darts at Bournemouth*. But you can see this for yourself in the above list.

But I am here with you today sorry could you change that to I am writing this for you today thank you where were we oh yes I am writing this for you today so that you will end by having some idea of the kind of ideas that we in the BBC are on the lookout for. We have a strong team of lively young people among them erm erm oh oh who the hell have we got okay scrub that just put lively young people whom we can rely on to turn our Fresh Ideas into ordinary programmes.

From Fresh Idea to Small Screen

We will learn a lot from following the making of one programme from paper to screen or from cradle to grave as it were.

The Beeb is always on the lookout for what we call Police Action Series.

Police Action Series are always in demand.

But the days of Dixon of Dock Green are long gone. Thirty years ago, dear old George Dixon would cure an offender for life by fetching him a sharp cuff across the neck. But these days he would probably prefer to shoot the wrong 'un stone dead. Tastes are changing all the time. That is what makes television such an exciting area to work in.

So let's say you've hit on the idea for a brand new Police Action Series.

Casebook: The Making of Smith and Jones

Idea Development

What kind of Police Action Series do you envisage?

Starsky and Hutch? No.

It's been done before. A fresh idea must be that. Fresh.

An English Starsky and Hutch? That's more like it.

But set in England?

Great idea.

At this stage, the production team would begin to get excited. But where in England exactly? I can see a long discussion, maybe two or three hours.

Then someone suggests London.

Brilliant. London is a big city with a lot of crime. Packed full of colourful characters to fill the minor roles. What do I mean when I say colourful characters question mark.

Characters with a bit of colour.

1. Vicars
2. Market tenders
3. Bartenders
4. People with moustaches
5. Fat people
6. Talkative cabbies
7. Busty Cockneys
8. City gents in bowler hats
9. Rolls-Royce drivers
10. Sinister men with no lines

By inserting colourful characters in their Police Action Series our BBC writers have earned themselves international reputations.

Naming the Series

Obviously we can't call our English Starsky and Hutch *Starsky and Hutch*. Too close to the original. How about two typically English names instead?

Smith and Jones springs to mind.

Perfect exclamation mark.

Plotting the Series

Police Action Series always begin with a hold-up.

Let's begin with a hold-up. Perhaps of a bullion van. Something a bit different.

Excellent opportunity for a car chase.

But the villains vanish into thin air. This gives an exciting twist to the first five minutes. 'This is a little different. Let's continue to watch,' the average viewer will exclaim.

Now we can afford a few words or dialogue as we call it in

the Beeb. Back to Smith and Jones – Smith is the one with the hat – in the office.

Their superior 'Supe' is hopping mad. He threatens to take them off the case.

Time for another hold-up.

Room for a car chase here.

The villains vanish into thin air. The signs point to the same gang. The viewer is gripped.

Our heroes Smith and Jones are really up against it.

The plot thickens. Jones gets himself a classy girlfriend and leaves her in a house by herself.

Supe finds out that Smith and Jones have decided to 'go it alone'.

He is hopping mad.

Good time for another car chase. This time someone is murdered.

'Looks like we've got a homicide on our hands,' says Smith to Jones.

Then Jones realises his classy girlfriend might be in danger.

Cut to girlfriend alone in house. She is being threatened by a masked man.

Cut to Smith and Jones car-chasing back to the house.

Cut to girlfriend screaming.

Cut to Smith and Jones.

At this stage the viewer will wish to know whether they will get to her in time.

Cut to house. Screams. Enter Smith and Jones. Masked intruder drops gun on floor. Who will get the gun question mark. Lot of punching. Jones pulls intruder's mask off.

It is Supe. Brilliant twist. No wonder he didn't want them to go it alone exclamation mark.

Last scene. Smith and Jones enjoying a drink with classy girlfriend who has regained her composure. Room for dialogue here. Smith cracks a joke. They all laugh. Nice to end on an up. The end.

Producing the Series

Casting
This is a matter of getting the right actor or actress for the right part.

Costumes
Obviously in a contemporary Police Action Series there is no room for the Period Costumes which have earned the BBC an International Reputation.

Filming
This requires the requisite number of technicians, cameramen, et cetera.

Post-production
This refers to everything that happens *after* the production.

Administration

As an administrator myself I know that 99.999% of any programme is administration. As I often say to my colleagues on the 'artistic' side of things, 'I received my OBE in 1974 for my administrative abilities.' A few personal anecdotes might give you an insight into the demands made upon an administrator.

1) When I first arrived at the Beeb back in the mists of time I was asked what is your flair question mark. I was not prepared for this one. I said, 'I don't have a flair.' And within less than a year I was Head of Internal Administration. Sometimes it pays to be honest.

2) I well remember the problems caused by the great Aberfan disaster. At the time I was in charge of External Broadcasting of Famines, Earthquakes and Royalty. The Queen was visiting the wrecked Welsh village, so I was placed in the hot seat. Precisely ten minutes to round up a minimum of five grieving mothers. Be tactful but forceful, I told my assistants. They arrived back in just three minutes with the full complement of stricken mums. 'Beautiful,' I said, 'but how did you do it question mark.' 'Told 'em Harry Secombe might be turning up,' they replied. The resultant news broadcast pulled all the awards in the annual ceremonies. This was most gratifying and afforded some small consolation to the victims and their families.

3) I modestly admit that I was the first man to introduce 'audience laughter' to television. Our export sales on Sir

Kenneth Clark's memorable *Civilisation* series had been poor. 'Lacks the light touch,' the reports came back from America, Japan and Scandinavia. But by adding laughter and billing it as a madcap romp by a snooty professor around the hilarious world of the upper crust we achieved record sales.

4) Most programme makers are also keen programme viewers. I find that television is a window on the world. By pressing a single button one can enter a world of people dying of starvation and by pressing it again one can laugh at the antics of Little and Large. Press it a third time and you can enjoy a car chase, and, if you're still not satisfied, you can press it again for a riot in South Africa. Great variety, and all for seventeen pence a day. Of course, watching it through the eyes of a pro makes me a little more critical. When I see the swollen head of a dying child I get irritated with the camera angle — and then it's over to Little and Large for me!

Current Affairs Administration

If you wish to bring a Fresh Idea to the BBC you must first know in what field you wish to work and I'm not talking about fields as in the countryside exclamation mark no I'm talking about contexts.

What are the different kinds of context? First, there's the Eurovision Song Context oh isn't it okay cancel it. My own context is really current affairs. I like to know what is going on in the world from an unbiased source.

Lack of Bias is Important
In the reporting of any dispute, we are keen not to take one side or the other. People all over the world look to us to tell them what an average BBC reporter on £18,500 a year with a mortgage and maybe a small family thinks about any given situation: they know that he won't have strong feelings one way or the other on any issue of major importance, and they respect him for it.

But so is News Selection too
Literally hundreds of different things happen in the world every day, and it would take hours to report them all.

This is where selection comes in.

Have you got what it takes to select the best news for each day question mark. This is the admission test we give to bright sparks who wish to make a career in the BBC newsroom.

TV News: Do You Have a Nose

There are no hard and fast rules. I do not pretend that there is only one right answer to these questions. Fashions in news coverage come and go. One man's car crash is another man's tug-of-love tot exclamation mark.

1) Imagine you are a high-powered television news executive. Place the following news items in order of merit. Reports come in on the following subjects:

a) 11 people including 3 children killed in car crash outside Swansea.

b) 500 people die in earthquake in Brazil. No Britons involved.

c) Prince Andrew opens new precinct in Hartlepool. 'I declare this precinct open!' he laughs good-naturedly. 600-strong crowd cheers.

d) 16 people plus 2 children die in bomb-blast in Londonderry. No Britons involved.

e) Pint-sized comedian Ronnie Corbett unhurt in motorway crash which kills 30.

f) 2000 factory workers laid off in Cliveden, Lancs, due to loss of major order. Planned royal visit cancelled.

g) War in Nicaragua escalates. No Britons involved.

h) And finally, Prince Edward took a turn at Caribbean dancing today when visiting a youth centre in Toxteth . . . before taking a right royal tumble!

(A rough guide: 5 Britons equal 50 Europeans or Americans or 5000 other nationalities. A child is worth 6 adults. A member of the Royal Family equals half a million Britons, 6 million Europeans or Americans and half the population of all other countries.)

REPORT: I would plump for (e). It has all the elements of a great news story. Laughter (Ronnie Corbett), Relief (unhurt) and a Few Tears (crash kills 30). Never lead with a war. Wars have a tendency to look the same and are not good television. I also like (d) though one must be on one's guard against saturation coverage of Northern Ireland — it's too often a cue for Little and Large.

2) Place in order of merit:
   a) The funeral of a tragic tot
   b) Policeman injured in race riot
   c) Funeral of a much-loved gran
   d) Horse dies on Derby Day

REPORT: Either (d) or (a) appeal to me. If the tot died in an appealing way that ties in with a topical debate (AIDS, nuclear fall-out, drug abuse) then great, but if the horse was owned by HM the Queen, obviously the horse comes first.

3) The preceding news item has involved an almost-human chimp owned by a tug-of-love tot whose foster-mother is claiming invalidity allowance from the European Court of Human Rights. Which of these reaction shots do you encourage the newscaster to adopt afterwards:
   a) Wry smile
   b) Cheery grin
   c) Bemused smirk
   d) Serious
   e) Blank
   f) Left eyebrow slightly raised

REPORT: (d). The news is a serious business, as lovely Selina Scott points out in her bestselling *It's News to Me!* (Arrow paperbacks).
   One of the most difficult tasks for any newsreader is to learn to adjust the fact to the right expression. A smile is no way to greet a motorway pile-up nor is a scowl appropriate to news of our Royal Family. At least two weeks of the three-month Newcasters' Training Course (run from a high-security base in Sandy, Berks) is spent tutoring the latest recruits in Facial Deportment. 'If in doubt — look serious,' says Sir Alistair Burnet in his traditional end-of-term lecture — and he's right.

4) You are the producer of *Question Time*, the top-rated discussion programme hosted by Sir Robin Day. Which of

these questions do you choose?

a) In the light of recent events, does the panel believe that a complete change of government policy is the only means of bringing about a solution that is fair to everyone?

b) Bearing in mind the news today, can the panel tell us what the news tomorrow will hold?

c) Does the panel have confidence in the present situation and, if not, what situation do they envisage in years to come?

d) Given that the vast majority of ordinary men and women are united in believing that they belong to the vast majority of ordinary men and women, could the panel please tell us whether, in the light of the day-to-day running of the country, we would be better served if the people concerned or their representatives got together around a table and held full and frank discussions OR would the panel prefer to see the upholding of decent standards of behaviour in an already tense and volatile situation as a means of showing our determination to carry on as normal as do the vast majority of ordinary men and women?

REPORT: (d) is the correct answer.

I have always been a believer in democracy no change that to I have always been a great believer in democracy and I sincerely believe in letting the ordinary men and women off the street have their say.

5) Twelve minutes into a half-hour news broadcast, your newsreader drops dead without warning. Do you:

a) carry on as normal using his face but someone else's voice?

b) Turn it into a thirty-second news item, using live footage, with unscripted commentary by substitute newscaster?

c) End the news there, leaving the viewers with the impression that this was the rehearsed light-hearted jest with which television news traditionally concludes?

d) Immediately send camera crew to wife's house in time for later news bulletin?

REPORT: The correct answer is (a). Without wishing to reveal too many tricks of the trade it is worth noting that one famous newscaster — who shall be nameless exclamation mark – died three months ago, but his producer saw this as no reason to terminate his career in television and he continues to cast the news at least twice a week.

6) You are a researcher sent to prepare suitable questions for the following types of people:
   i)   The captain of a winning soccer team
   ii)   The grief-stricken mother of an earthquake victim
   iii)   A man who has just gained the world record for spaghetti-eating
   iv)   A candidate who has just lost a marginal by-election
   v)   The captain of a lifeboat whose six-man crew has drowned saving a loveable pooch

Match these possible questions with the above people:
   a) How do you feel?
   b) How do you feel?
   c) How do you feel?
   d) How do you feel?
   e) How do you feel?

REPORT: Trick question. Each of these questions is the most suitable: they are all the same. 'How do you feel?' says it all in four simple words.

As you can see if you have your finger on the hot-house of Current Affairs there are one hundred and one different decisions to be made and ethics is just as important as camera angles.

Documentary Administration

Documentaries are an essential part of the Beeb's Current Affairs output. In Current Affairs the need for Fresh Ideas isn't so important. Who needs Fresh Ideas when there are hundreds dying every day on your doorstep question mark. But Fresh Ideas are always needed in our Documentary division.
   Here are just some of the recent documentaries we have produced which started life as Fresh Ideas:
   The Problems of the Inner City
   The Problems facing British Rail
   The Problems Facing Us at Home

Consumer Problems
The Problems Facing the Tourist Industry
General Problems

As you can see by a cursory glance over this list, our Documentaries Unit has a reputation for hard-hitting investigations of the issues of the day. But they also like to have a go at less world-shattering events and ideas, and our half-hour Sunday slot, *Touching on the Truth*, provides an excellent forum for these smaller items. It's amazing how much ground you can cover in 'the half hour', and a fresh guest presenter provides additional interest and variety. Here are just some of our recent productions:

Anyone Up There? – Judith Chalmers asks, 'Is there a God?'

The Next Step – Peter France investigates belief in an afterlife.

Naughty! Naughty! – Taking a break from *Holiday '87*, Chris Kelly asks, 'What is the nature of Evil?'

The Art of the Matter – Libby Purves gives a personal view of the cross-fertilisation between abstract and representational art in the second half of the twentieth century, with music by Lance Percival.

Hang On a Minute – Bernie Winters shows us his more serious side when he chairs a studio debate on the return of capital punishment with the irrepressible Freddie Starr and boffin Paul Johnson.

Whither the Future? – Melvyn Bragg examines future developments in politics and the arts with contributions from, among others, Bernard Falk, Clive James, Russell Davies and Craig Raine.

The History of Western Philosophy – Under the watchful eye of Norris Macwhirter, Richard Baker plots a course through this difficult terrain – and all in thirty minutes!

Justice – Is Britain's adversarial system really the best means of establishing guilt or innocence? Panel game with Miles Kington and Barry Cryer.

The Existence of Hell – Esther and the team ask you the public what you think hell will be like – and come up with some surprising and hilarious answers!

Time to Think – From the Bible to Borges, man has always been fascinated by the nature of Time. Now find out just what Cilla thinks when Cilla Black returns to our screens this autumn.

As you can see, the 'Beeb' has come up with a series of thought-provoking half-hours to which all the members of the family can relate.

I hope that this has encouraged you to consider the merits of a career in Broadcasting.

I for one can't imagine life without that box in the corner of the living room. I have learned all I know about life and about people from the television, and I can remember quite a lot of it. Here are just five things I have learned from my 'telly':

1)
2)
3)
4)
5)

If you could just fill in five interesting facts from some book or other I'd be very grateful and that should bring us up to the amount of words they want by the way what's on telly tonight question mark.

Name

Penny de Rennie

Date of birth

I feel 17

Profession

Health, Love and Fitness Consultant

Position currently held

Lotus: essential for healthy bowel movement.

Family

I'm lucky, my husband is also my lover – or at least was when he was still my husband.

Achievements to date

In my premier volume, *In the Raw*, I taught the world to eat raw vegetables and experience a wide variety of sex with many different people. The follow-up, *In the Raw Reconsidered*, alerted the world to the dangers of promiscuity and the cancer peril that may well lie in some uncooked vegetables.

   On a more personal level, I have become a complete woman – healthy living and healthy loving.

Awards

I'm in love with life – isn't that enough?

High point of career

Meeting Shirley Conran, and later becoming close friends with that amazing lady.

Low point of career

In 1978, I was a fatty. I smoked 80 cigarettes a day. I ate only fatty products. My boyfriend used to beat me – and I never noticed.

Best friend

Shirley Conran. She's taught me all I know, and that's saying one helluva lot.

What makes you happy

Not eating, not drinking, not smoking.

What makes you sad

Not being happy.

What qualities do you look for in a human being

Non-smoking; in love with life; preferably Aries; idealistic; open —
and a great sense of humour.

Most memorable disaster

The Titanic I suppose.

Heroes

Clare Rayner. She *understands*.

Ambitions

To market my own line in Penny de Rennie Heart Disease
Monitoring Kits with full Penny de Rennie motif, in dynamic blue
and gold with free scalpel — out next year hopefully.

If you weren't yourself who would you choose to be

In England, Felicity Kendal. In America, Erica Jong.

Pets if any

I keep tapes of whales singing for relaxation purposes. Mankind can learn one heck of a lot from dolphins – how to swim, and so on.

Hobbies

Healthy living, healthy loving; reading mind-expanding and body-reducing books; not smoking; lending a shoulder to cry on.

Religious convictions if any

God is within me; He is I; you are what you eat; I am mainly raw carrot and low-fat yoghurt.

Favourite book

Anything with 'This Book Will Change Your Life' on the cover.

If you had three wishes what would they be

1. More lettuce.
2. That everyone could be like me.
3. An end to cigarette advertising at sports events.

What would you most like to be remembered for

Countless acts of generosity to small people, many of which have not yet been reported by the media.

Pet hate

Apartheid and people smoking in restaurants, but mainly people smoking in restaurants.

Favourite catchphrase

You are what you eat, and you are not what you leave on the side of your plate.

Are you frightened of death and if so why

Who's going to die?

Your Body is Your Best Friend

says PENNY de RENNIE, author of In the Raw *and* In the Raw Reconsidered.

Hi!

You know something? When I walk down the street, men's heads turn. No kidding. In the last fortnight, I've had firm proposals of marriage from the most fascinating men. A leading neurologist. An expert in scuba-diving. Two Nobel Peace Prize-winners. A Chief Constable. A landscape painter. The head of one of our major merchant banks. Even a Catholic priest!

You know what they say? They tell me that I am All Woman and that I make them feel All Man. They desire me for my body and for myself.

Not bad for a 48-year-old with knock-knees, a small moustache, two types of venereal disease and a bad cold, huh?

And I'll let you in on a secret. I'm shy as anything.

So how does the bitch do it, I hear you ask?

It's a secret. But it's a secret that I want to share.

With you. And you. And you. And you. And you.

I'll tell you how to treat your body like a shrine and have men – fascinating men, beautiful men, wealthy men, MANLY men – worship at it morning noon and night.

And you don't have to pay them a cent.

Chapter One
CUT THOSE EXTRA POUNDS, FATTY!

Think you'll get a wealthy merchant banker in the sack with a body like that?

No way!

Men are allowed to be flabby. It goes with power and self-confidence – and all that lovely money.

Whoever heard of a Flabby Woman?

Count me out!

You've gotta lose pounds and pounds before those eyes are gonna turn as you walk down the street. And that means SELF-CONTROL.

Not a word in your vocabulary, huh? Well it soon will be, or I'm not Penny de Rennie.

The PR Plan Diet

Shed pounds the PR way – and eat as much as you like!

Sounds impossible? Not at all. Take a look at my two illustrations. On the right, we see a woman before the weight loss programme – and on the left we see the same woman *after* – and she has lost a full 6 pounds WITHOUT LOSING A MOUTHFUL OF FOOD.

BEFORE   AFTER

Hear this. Since the operation, the lady has been dated by a top theatrical costumier, a world-famous gynaecologist, one of Fleet Street's most distinguished columnists and someone extremely big in the advertising industry. Kinda impressive, huh?

I'd like to tell you of another friend of mine. Let's call her Kay. Men found her a turn-off.

Her breasts were pert.

Her legs long and slender.

Her neck like a swan's.

Her bottom petite and inviting.

So what was the problem?

Her face. Horrid, horrid, horrid.

She came to me with her problem. What should she do, she asked.

Get rid of it, I said.

But *how?* she asked.

The PR Plan Diet, I said.

BEFORE   AFTER

Hear this. Since the operation, the lady has been to bed with a fire chief, the head window-dresser at one of our leading department stores, a company director and the surgeon himself. Not bad for a girl who thought she lacked confidence, eh?

Of course, there are old-fashioned molls who throw up their hands when it comes to cutting off limbs.

Here's a secret. Promise not to tell?

I'm a bit like that myself. So I take it easy, and count my calories in the Fergie Diet.

Here goes!

The Fergie Diet

NEVER EAT:
While scuba-diving
During intercourse
While asleep
At a funeral
During your own marriage service
During an operation
While parachuting
TRY NOT TO EAT:
Flavoured glue
All varieties of garden shrub
Animals in the zoo except rabbits and possibly squirrels
Parts of yourself
Pins
Expensive cushions
Structural parts of buildings
Hardback books
Cooking implements
EAT ONLY OCCASIONALLY:
Dead flies
Cakes still in their wrappings
Coal
Squezy bottles
Used editions of the *Radio Times*
Your teeth
Bread shops
Mice OR rats in their skin
Your best friend
Your tongue

Why not try these simple exercises?

Friends tell me they wish they could exercise in public but that they *just don't dare*. Nonsense I say!

Whenever seated in a bus, I raise and lower my buttock muscles 10 times every 30 seconds. They are now so tense and rounded that I have attracted, in the last fortnight, a senior Queen's Counsel, the owner of a wine bar, a prominent stationmaster, a football manager and a modern poet. And all for the cost of a bus fare!

a) Before the buttocks are clenched.

b) Following the clenching of buttocks. The rest of the public carry on unaware.

Surreptitious clenching and unclenching of hair follicles can prove effective in the quest for perfect grooming.

Private exercises are better suited to the inhibited. Go wild behind closed doors!

Why not stand on your pretty little head?

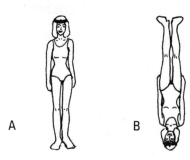

A   B

But do remember to return to a normal posture when friends enter or they might think that you have grown two necks and two foot-shaped heads – spooky!

'Course, there are kooky rich guys out there who go for gals with those kinda heads!

If that's the case, my advice is: KEEP THOSE FEET IN THE AIR, DARLING! One of my dearest friends – let's call her Irene – was doing this very exercise when the millionaire widower from the luxury penthouse upstairs put his head round the door. I can tell you this – when he set eyes on Irene he POSITIVELY FLIPPED!

To cut a long story short, they've been married now for two whole years and Irene is the delighted owner of two apartments –

one in New York, one in LA – a country retreat in North Dakota PLUS pocket money of 500,000 dollars per year.

Not bad for a little girl from Wyoming, huh?

Irene's big dread is that Hank – that's Mr Moneybags – will somehow find out all is not as it seems and what he thinks are two sexy weirdo heads are just those little tootsies stuck in the air. But with all that lovely money, she can afford some truly amazing gadgetry and couturiery to disguise her normality. Let's snatch a look at how she goes about it:

Irene and Hank in their First Anniversary Commemoration Photograph (note cross-section showing that Irene is, unbeknownst to Frank, standing on her head: the mechanical trolley appliance, affording access to easy movement, is operated by her mouth)

I once asked Irene – loudmouth! – how come Hank didn't guess something was up when they were in the sack together.

'Guess he just thinks I'm low-slung,' was her reply.

MEN: *Give 'em what they want, and they'll ask no questions!*

MEN: *Once they're turned on – keep them turned on!*

I had another dear friend – I'll call her Samantha ('cos that was her name!!) who could never get a man.

Poor Samantha.

She tried everything, and I mean *everything*.

Losing weight

Putting on weight

Stilettoes

Suspenders

Boxer shorts

Pretending to be clever

Rubber gear

Pretending to be a frog.

She even wrapped herself in a thin white paper and lit the end 'cos she knew her guy liked smoking.

But still she couldn't catch her man.

As a last resort, she tried a five-hour mudpack beauty treatment, covering all her pretty face for five hours with this gooey mud substance.

Yuk!

She's been at it for three hours and twenty-two minutes when there's a ring on the bell.

Cripes!

Who can it be? She can't ruin her last-resort-treatment now!

'Who is it?' she asks over the ansa-phone.

'Jerry,' comes the reply.

Oh no! Jerry's the guy the Just Browzing Companions Agency sent – and she forgot he was coming!!! What can she do? She can't send him away – and with the mudpack on her face she can't admit him!

'D'y'mind waiting outside about one hour thirty-eight minutes, please Jerry?'

'Well – I – er – it's mighty cold out here, Samantha.'

'Chhhh – gosh!' says Samantha. 'Okay then' – and she presses the bleeper.

So Jerry comes in to be confronted with Samantha's face completely covered in sticky, gooey, bumpy mud – even her eyes!

'Sorry 'bout this,' Samantha stammers.

Jerry's mouth is wide open.

'I said I'm sorry. P'raps you'd better go now – just like all the others.'

'You look –' says Jerry.

'Don't say it – I know,' sighs Samantha.

'Beautiful. Real – beautiful!' gasps Jerry.

'I do?' says Samantha through the mud.

'You do,' says Jerry, 'I've never seen a face like yours before. It's . . . beautiful. Will you take dinner with me, please, Samantha?'

Other guys have brought hip-flasks or gum around before, but NO ONE has ever asked her out for dinner.

'Why, sure,' she replies. 'Give me two minutes to get ready, Jerry.'

In one minute fifteen seconds she's back wearing a slinky number – and the mudpack.

No dumb cookie, our Samantha!

Here's a lovely shot of the two of them at that very candle-lit dinner in a cute little Spanish pizzeria Jerry knew well:

Jerry and Samantha at Jose's Pizzeria, East 52nd Street

So it turns out that Jerry owns his own chain of computer showrooms, dabbles in real estate and has a part-share in three successful pop groups – and he asks Samantha to marry him before she's even finished her Four Seasons.

That was six years ago. They're now happily married with their own swimming pool – and Samantha still hasn't removed that mudpack!

MOTTO: Guys are great big babies: play along with 'em and you'll both be happy!

Don't agree? Well, just consider a couple of things:

Your man likes to dress up in diapers, right?

And he likes to shake a rattle too, right?

And he sucks a dummy after you've finished intercourse, right?

And you're still telling me he ain't a great big overgrown baby?

Come off it, honey! Who's kiddin' who?

There's one thing to remember about babies. They'll do anything for fun and games!

If they don't get fun and games – they start to wail!

And they like *new* fun and *fresh* games *all the time*: that boring old bear might keep 'em quiet for an hour or two, but soon they'll be asking for toys that buzz and whirr and fly and squeal and bubble.

And you're not going to deny them *that*, are you?

'Course you're not!

How to Keep Your Man Happy in Bed

I'd like to tell you about Roger and Jenny. Married four years. Both attractive, outgoing human beings. And very much in love. But one thing was wrong: they weren't having fun in bed any more. Roger just seemed to have lost interest. Jenny was worried. Very worried. She knew that a man who wasn't having fun in her bed would soon be having fun in someone else's. Wise girl.

'Have you tried 69?' I quizzed her.

'Well, er, – no,' she admitted.

'Have you tried doggie-fashion?' I persevered.

'To be honest, Penny – no,' she replied.

'You haven't!' I exclaimed.

I put that right in no time!

These days, Jenny tells Roger he looks younger than 69 and then dresses their pooch up in all the latest styles, and the pair of them go to sleep with smiles all over their faces. Another marriage saved, courtesy Penny de Rennie!

How to Keep Your Man Happy Around the House

So you're happy in bed. Get along fine. Great.

But what about those eighteen hours a day (average) you're outta bed? Not so hot, huh?

I don't know what kinda job your man is involved in. Maybe he's a safety controls inspector, the press officer to an amusement and leisure park, an insurance claims investigator or a leading hotelier. But what I do know is this:

NO MAN LIKES TO LIVE IN A TIP.

And guess whose duty it is to make sure your home looks as spick and span as Versailles, the famous palace of the emperors of France?

Don't turn the other way – it's *you* I'm talking to. If your house is a tip no man's gonna stay with you.

Dreary, huh? But necessary? Right!

A lot of women waste a lot of time doing the RIGHT chores the WRONG way. Or, doing the WRONG chores the RIGHT way. I've even known real tramps and thickos doing the WRONG chores the WRONG way – but that's another story!

You could do with some labour-saving hints, huh? Here goes!

- CRUSHED fish-heads make effective and UNUSUAL table mats.
- Never DISCARD a brussel sprout. They make EXCELLENT arm-cushions for the WEARY DESK-WORKER.
- STAINS ON THE WALL can be fascinating. Why not give each one a felt-tip FRAME?
- AVOID MILK BUBBLING OVER. Never use the cooker.
- Old milk bottles smashed up can deter BABY from crawling too close to the FIRE.
- GET RID of wine stains on your FAVOURITE CARPET by cutting out the offending SECTION with SCISSORS.
- What to do with OLD BRILLO PADS? Answer in one word – EARRINGS. But first remove the *gunge*!
- BATH PLUGS can be used to great effect for KEEPING WATER in your bath.

You have just saved yourself one heckuva lotta time, wifey!

But there's more to being a woman than just housework and beddy-byes.

You got it in one – conversation.

No guy wants to come home after a busy day to a little lady who's got nothin' to say for herself.

Gee, that's the biggest turn-off of 'em all!

So whaddya say?

Easy. Just study this handy checklist of fascinating topics. One a day, huh? It runs on a twenty-day cycle.

I know what you're thinking. But don't worry – at the end of twenty days, your guy won't remember a thing you told him before, so off you go again!

He says: Hi! Darling! I'm home!
   You say: Hi! Darling! How was work?
   He says: Oh, so-so! Could I do with a drink!
   You say: Let me get you one darling!
   He says: Why thanks honey!
You say:

DAY 1: *Which do you consider the greater lyric poet, honey – William Wordsworth or Samuel Taylor Coleridge?*

DAY 2: *They're saying it costs millions of pounds to put a man into space, honey.*

DAY 3: *Is it true that bulls are in fact colour-blind, honey?*

DAY 4: *Lynda Lee-Potter argues that drugs offenders should be jailed for life. Where do you stand on this thorny problem, honey?*

DAY 5: *They're saying the exhibits in Madame Tussaud's are only waxworks, honey.*

DAY 6: *I guess J.R. just isn't to be trusted, eh, honey?*

DAY 7: *How in the world does one go about splitting an atom, honey?*

DAY 8: *Honey, what's a 'gourmet'?*

DAY 9: *Honey, when they say 'stir gently' on this packet, what do they mean exactly?*

DAY 10: *Honey, are you a Jungian at all?*

DAY 11: *Honey, let's get away from it all! Let's go stay at the Crossroads Motel for a change!*

DAY 12: *Why are plants green, honey?*

DAY 13: *Honey, do you find the Black and White Minstrels racially offensive and if so would you have them banned?*

DAY 14: *Honey, can biography ever be an art form?*

DAY 15: *Honey, do you agree with Paul Johnson in this morning's newspaper when he argues for greater bugging of subversives rather than less?*

DAY 16: *What is the difference between a 'hardcover' and a 'paperback', honey?*

DAY 17: *Honey, what is an 'oboe'?*

DAY 18: *Honey, would you say that the pursuit of happiness is incompatible with the pursuit of truth – or not?*

DAY 19: *Honey, do you agree when they say that some sparkling white wines compare favourably with many champagnes?*

DAY 20: *Honey, what do they mean when they say, 'as different as chalk and cheese'?*

Happy talking!
Happy playing!
And remember – Your Body is Your Best Friend!

Penny de Rennie

© *Penny de Rennie Inc.*

Name

Chris P. Rice

Date of birth

20–5–46. Born Chris de Rice.
Dropped the 'de', 1966. I hate erecting barriers, you know?

Profession

Jerk-of-all-Trades — and Master of 'em too!

Position currently held

Legs crossed, hand scratching bonce. Seriously — I've always
been independent of hierarchical structures. I'm not into the
power-kick, frankly.

Family

Don't talk to me about me younger bruvver Tim, famous sod
though he is (!). There's also me wife Jill and (nudge! nudge!)
'lovely lady' Jacqui de Reuben (breathe not a word!).

Achievements to date

How long have you got?!

Awards

I'm not that kinda guy. I don't *need* formal approval, thank you very much.

High point of career

When the then Simon Dee walked into my then boutique in '66 and ordered one hundred cowboy hats, I was pretty bloody chuffed, no kidding.

Low point of career

Dee brought them back the next day, no explanation, nothing.

Best friend

Me teddy-bear Fred! No – seriously, wife Jill is a source of great strength, and I have a soft spot (if you can call it that!) for my 'leading lady' Jacqui.

What makes you happy

Making love to a beautiful woman.

What makes you sad

Stopping making love to a beautiful woman.

What qualities do you look for in a human being

Warmth. A terrific sense of humour. Commitment. Friendship. And maybe a bit of ready cash in their pocket?

Most memorable disaster

Must be the time I went skiing with Uncle Mike Read, great guy. We both had our eyes (and much else besides) on one helluva beautiful chick. Got her back to our chalet – turns out it's a bloke in drag! Red faces time!

Heroes

James Hendrix, musician and lovely man, R.I.P.
The late great Buddy Holly, R.I.P.

Ambitions

To grow internally.
To keep on keeping on, as the songster put it.

If you weren't yourself who would you choose to be

Jimmy Savile, OBE. In my book, the man's a saint.

Pets if any

Saucy! Seriously, we've got a cat called Bolan and a goldfish called Janis, both of 'em a lot of fun.

Hobbies

Windsurfing. Chess. Picking me nose. Making love to beautiful women.

Religious convictions if any

I believe in something, call it God, call it Nature, call it Humanity, call it what you will. It's the feeling you get when you wake up and the sun's shining. It's the feeling you get when you're dancing with a lovely lady to a song by Bowie. It's the feeling you get when you first read *The Hobbit*. I don't need to go to church to prove anything though. It's between me and the man they called Jesus who is basically the same as the bloke they called Buddha. It's a very personal, very precious thing.

Favourite book

Lord of the Rings by J. R. R. Ewing. *The Doors of Perception* by R. D. Laing. Anything by Craig Raine.

If you had three wishes what would they be

1. To have another three!!
2. To meet David Puttnam – he's done so much to revive the British film industry, plus I've got an outline he'd be interested in!
3. To make a classic video and write a classic hit song – whoops, sorry, that's four!

What would you most like to be remembered for

My line from my song 'They Died Too Young' which goes:

When Mama Cass began to sing
She sprayed gold paint over everything

For me, it says it all.

Pet hate

The West End theatre scene. Snobs. Cynics. People who force their beliefs upon me. Intellectual snobs who don't see the pop lyric as an art form like any other. Fascism of any kind. Record companies (see previous sentence). Ladies who say no.

Favourite catchphrase

How was it for you?

Are you frightened of death and if so why

No. It's the last great adventure – and anyway I'll be able to meet Jayne Mansfield in heaven!

Fashion
F-F-F-F-Fashion
Fashion
F-F-F-F-Fashion
Fashion

(from 'Fashion' by David Bowie)

Those lyrics by the great Bowie say it all, I think you'll agree. Since that late, great year 1965 – remember 1965? Course you do! – I've been keeping my head above water and earning a crust by staying abreast of fashion.

How do I do it? Frankly, old chum, I wish I knew. Call it fortune-telling. Call it being Thoroughly Modern. Call it having my finger on the pulse of this Crazy Planet. Your guess, et cetera . . .

Best thing I can do is to 'talk you thru' the various stages in my career-cum-universe, throwing you and yours the odd tip along the journey. I've changed – and I'm talking now *as a person* – every year of my weird and wonderful life. I've never wanted to get into the establishment thing of grey men with grey wives and two-and-a-quarter children or whatever. For me, every year's different.

I could rap on like this for literally years – I'm the original gab merchant. But let's go straight into my (almost) year-by-year look at what was happening and where your friend and mine Chris P. Rice was at.

We kick off in the Sixties. What a literally amazing error that was: the error of the Beatles and the Stones, the error of free love and anti-war, the error when we let it all hang out – literally!

1965: The Error of Photography

You just had to be a photographer if you were young and in London and it was 1965. Everywhere you went, people were making love and taking photographs of each other. You'll probably remember my exhibition at the Purple Place Gallery. I shared it with an unknown young photographer called David Bailey – and look what became of him! (He died in a motorbike accident: the well-known David Bailey was someone different.) I exhibited 20 photographs, all in black and white, thus lending the title to the show – 'Black and White'. You might get some ideas for your own snaps by perusing the catalogue:

1) Tramp One
2) Tramp Two
3) Tramp Three
4) Demolished building One
5) Demolished building Two
6) Demolished building Three
7) Sky
8) Earth
9) Earth and Sky

10) Earth and Sky and Penelope
11) Penelope with Flower
12) Bird in flight
13) Fat couple on beach
14) Social Comment (Refuse collectors, Margate)
15) Broken bottle
16) Penelope exploring herself

CATALOGUE NOTE: THESE PHOTOGRAPHS ARE ALL IN BLACK AND WHITE. THE THEME IF THERE IS A THEME IS CONTRASTS. CONTRASTS BETWEEN OLD AND NEW, PEOPLE AND PLACES, YOU AND ME. I HAVE BEEN INFLUENCED IN THIS WORK BY MANY FRIENDS INCLUDING THE SPIRIT OF WILLIAM BLAKE, JIMMY THE SODA-SYPHON, PENELOPE, MY GOOD FRIEND THE TRAMP, THE MUSIC OF DAVE CLARK, CHOPIN, THE STREETS, TALL JUDY AND EVERYONE WHO LIVES AND BREATHES ON THIS PLANET.

This is what I learned about photography:

a) Get yourself a good camera.

b) Always pick a great angle: low down can be brilliant.

c) Wait until you've got the perfect shot before pressing the shutter.

d) Every subject is different, unless it's the same subject.

e) Contrast is always interesting.

But by December, I was hanging up my Affelblad 907, ready for:

1966: The Error of the Boutique

It's now quite well known that I was the third person in London to wear a kipper tie, pretty outrageous at the time. What the hell, we were young and at the vanguard of a revolution that would leave the world a different place, a utopia where whoever wanted to wear a kipper tie was allowed to wear a kipper tie.

Borrowing the necessary dough from my good friend Harry Kircudbright (Lord Henry Kircudbright, if you will, but at the time he didn't want to take advantage) I opened 'I Was Queen Victoria's Purple Doughnut' on Carnaby Street in May '66. The interior was all orange and it was the first boutique where if you wanted to you could just sit and rap and if you wanted any of the clothes you just gave whatever you could afford. It closed in June, and in July we opened the legendary 'Kick Out The Jams', where all the helpers were dressed as whatever jam they felt reflected their being on that day – grapefruit, strawberry, raspberry and blackcurrant or whatever. Ringo Starr used to buy his kaftans from us, and Simon Dee once came in and ordered one hundred leather cowboy hats, I kid you not. I was the fifth person in London to wear a pink polo-neck, and the fourth to sell Emperor Rosko a psychedelic cravat.

After 'Kick Out The Jams' closed that September, we opened 'Free', a whole new concept with mirrors all over the walls and ceiling, loud music playing – and I mean loud – and just empty hangers where other boutiques had clothes. Over the entrance, we had this placard in psychedelic colours saying 'INVISIBLE CLOTHES FOR THE WORLD' and everyone really got off on that, helping themselves to the invisible clothes and paying us invisible money.

Lord Harry sold his stately pile to the Trusthouse Forte people ten years ago and now does something in the City; 'Free' is now a kiosk selling models of Beefeaters to tourists, and whatever happened to Simon Dee?

ALL WHITE – NO PROPS

Fig. 1. Interior Design for my 'Nothin' Doin'' boutique. Never got off the ground, though way ahead of its time.

1967: The Error of Imported Indian Craftwork

From being the fifth person in London to wear a pink polo-neck, it was just a short step to becoming the seventh person to get into India in a big way – and this was months before the Beatles commercialised it.

A short history of the Joss Stick

Literally, I've had some of my deepest thoughts while listening to Joss Sticks. The earth, you see, is this amazing, well, globe really, on which all these thousands, no, millions of people are living, and some are good and some are not so good but they're all living on this weird place together so they've got to learn to love one another and take care of Number One. This is the sort of thing I first felt when Regovan, brother of Donovan, came into 'Free' one day wearing a joss stick in his hair. I wanted to know more. And *now*.

Turns out that the joss stick originated in India literally hundreds of years ago and it's been there ever since. When you smell the aroma of joss you are immediately transported back in some mystical way through the mists of time to the last time you smelt joss, and you know that all over the world there are literally hundreds of people smelling joss *at exactly the same time*. Talk about blew my mind out in a car.

I never got to India but instead I opened 'Nice Karma' on the Tottenham Court Road, or just off it. After we were inundated with requests for second-hand Jags, I changed the name to 'Things Eastern Mainly'.

Ravi Shankar came round once but didn't buy anything. Things India taught me and the Beatles:

a) I am you
b) and you are me
c) and we are all together
d) but who's he?

1967 kinda melted into 1968, when lots happened but not in India or the Tottenham Court Road. Then we drifted into

1969: The Error of Drug Dealing

baked beans are green salad dressing is strawberry starfish the carrot is growing out of my knee the banana is yellow as the sun which shines on sliced white bread slice slice slice slice slice slice slice slice slice slice slice slice aaaagh please don't slice me I'm not a piece of bread I'm a human being

That was a prose-poem I wrote while completely out of my head on acid sitting in my folk's larder in March 1969. It turned into a pretty bad trip and I think the prose-poem conveys at least some of my anguish. But at the same time it opened up whole new worlds and it made me realise that nothing that seemed to be like it was was really the same way as we'd always taken it to be. For instance, acid taught me that

a) Human beings can fly or at least would be able to if they were birds.

b) Your mind is the same mind as my mind only your mind is yours and mine is mine.

c) That hat on top of your head – is it an octopus?

d) Birth and death are two words for the same thing.

Around June 1969, me and a few other guys who were really into acid hitched up this plan to liberate the Establishment by infiltrating ten tons of acid into a Buckingham Palace garden party. All those grey men freaking out and making love! But we didn't ever get it together. Shame.

Anyway in December 1969 both Janis Joplin and someone I met once called Big Keef died of drugs. The dream was over. It was the end of an error. The Seventies loomed.

1970: The Error of Depression

Everything that happened in 1970 was incredibly depressing, incredibly.

It was as if the balloon of love and peace that was the sixties had finally sunk. 1970 was arguably the worst year ever in the history of the human race. Altamont, Vietnam, Aberfan, the Kray Brothers, Watergate, the Profumo Affair, the Suez crisis, the death of Hendrix, the assassination of Kennedy, the break-up of the Beatles – it all happened in 1970, I could've sworn.

And some creep nicked my worry beads.

I spent the year in bed with a cup of instant coffee and no chick.

It was that kind of year. The kind that lasts and lasts.

And then along came Bowie.

1973: The Error of Bisexuality

Let's face it, we are all 50 per cent female, except for women that is, and they're 50 per cent male. Sure I fancy chicks. But I fancy blokes too. I fancy both. And it took a genius like Bowie to make me see it.

There's a starman
Waiting in the sky
He'd like to come and see us
But he thinks he'd blow our minds

The guy's a visionary. He's talking about interplanetary exploration (physical and spiritual), he's talking about the need for patience ('waiting'), he's talking about mental attitudes and the shock of the new ('thinks he'd blow our minds'), he's talking about dreams unfulfilled, and he's talking, perhaps most importantly of all, about himself, Bowie, part human being, part . . . what? Woman? In those brief four lines he manages to say more about life than a group like the Bay City Rollers managed to say in half a dozen.

Throughout 1973, I experimented with all kinds of sex. Guys. Girls. Guys 'n' girls. By the end of the year, I had come to terms with my own sexuality: I was equally unattractive to both men and women. 'The Jean Genie lives on his back,' sang Bowie. My song.

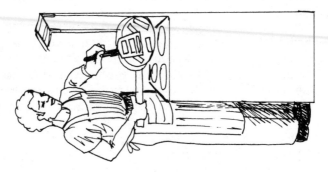

'The Jean Genie Lives on His Back'
Fig. 2: The Jean Genie cooks some fish fingers for his lunch.

After an experimental sex session in November I slipped a disc and had to take it easy until

1974: The Error of Investigative Journalism

While we had been bopping our hearts out to Sweet and Bowie the rest of the world was starving to death or worse. In 1974, Social Conscience hit me in a big way. 'Let me take you by the hand,' sang Ralph McTell, 'And lead you thru the streets of London, I'll show you something la da di da di da.' Talk about striking a chord.

There are literally hundreds of people who don't want to let the rest of us know what they are doing.

☞ Rain forests are cutting into the ozone level

☞ Every time you use an aerosol, the Chinese people jump up and down all at the same time

☞ There are far more Chinese people than there are people in all London combined

☞ The complete annihilation of London in 1967 was successfully predicted by Nostradamus centuries ago – but the British government has never acknowledged it

☞ The Loch Ness Monster was officially sighted in Dallas on 22 November 1963, the day they killed Kennedy

---

1975: The Error of the Frisbee

Basically, the frisbee is a masterpiece of simple design:

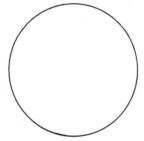

Illustration A: The frisbee

It is best employed in a field or grassy space:

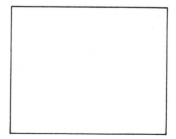

Illustration B: A field or grassy space

Instructions: It is best thrown between three (3) people:

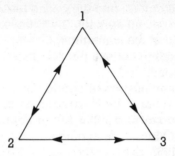

Illustration C: A frisbee being thrown between three (3) people

The beauty of the frisbee lies in its simplicity. In 1975, when I popularised it in Britain, it appealed to a nation which wanted to free its brain from all the financial and political muddles of the preceding year.

Frisbee is now officially recognised as a religion, thus becoming the first sport to qualify for that status. Its adherents, many of them influenced, like yours truly, by India in 1967, have discovered that many of the loose ends of Buddhism are tied up by throwing the Vishnu Fris Bee. In its eternal simplicity lies its spirituality. In many ways it's a variation on the ancient Australian boomerang, but with one major advance – it doesn't come back.

1977: The Error of Fringe Theatre

Chris P. Rice is for many people a name inseparable from The Theatre Next To The Toilet, at the Old Bull and Bush pub in East Cheam.

In fringe, you know your work is *really* powerful when the whole world keeps its distance, and the citizens of East Cheam showed how frightened they were of the raw realities by staying away from The Theatre Next To The Toilet in their hundreds.

A YEAR IN FRINGE

January 1977:
Don't Eat The Guinea-Pig. An agit-prop drama by the East Cheam collective showing how the guinea-pig comes to be on the East Cheam family dinner-table each Sunday lunch. It raises profound questions about the role of the guinea-pig in modern society.
'A scathing indictment' *Time Out*

February 1977:
Empty Space in the Dark. An experimental drama with no actors, sound or lights.
'Bleak and compelling' *Time Out*

March 1977:
Zzzzzzzzzz. Once upon a time, sex and death were the great taboos in our society. Olga Kitel mimes being asleep, followed by discussion.
'Essential' *Time Out*

April 1977:
The East Cheam Martyrs. A drama-documentary restaging the events of 1455 when five men and one woman from roughly the area of East Cheam, living in houses without electricity or running water, were driven by conditions beyond their control to murder their own children.
'Darkly compelling' *Time Out*

May 1977:
Hamlet by William Shakespeare. The Penis-Envy Feminist Collective Drama Theatre Workshop take a fresh look at the male menopause.
'Disturbing and strangely moving' *Time Out*

June 1977:
The Festival of International Dance and Movement. More than three dancers from no less than two international countries including Britain celebrate the body in all its aspects to the music of human breath. With Penny de Rennie.
'A revelation' *Time Out*

July 1977:
David Bowie Live in Concert.
'Incomparably better than the more famous David Bowie' *Time Out*

August 1977:
End Game by Samuel Beckett. A new production by Chris P. Rice. 'To me, Beckett's humour is often highlighted at the

expense of his more depressing insights into the human condition. This production aims to show that even his few jokes aren't really funny' – Chris P. Rice.

'Darkly black' *Time Out*

September 1977:

Charles Manson Benefit Evening. All artistes will be giving their services free.

October 1977:

You'll Wish You Never Came (253 minutes, no interval). Theatre-going is a bourgeois pursuit indulged in by those who exploit the proletariat.

'Uncomfortable and horribly honest' *Time Out*

November 1977:

International Festival of Mime. Scandinavian mime-artist Chrisvj P. Riht demonstrates what it is like to be stuck in an invisible box for three hours. Plus his hilarious 'Man in a Bus Queue'.

'Spare and pungent' *Time Out*

December 1977:

Christmas Pantomime: Jack and the Beanstalk. Unsuitable for children.

'Savage and macabre' *Time Out*

Fig. 3: Chrisvj P. Riht stars in his mime 'Absence'.

1978: The Error of Cheap Travel

Freddie Laker. Now, there's a name to conjure with! In 1978, he infected one helluva lot of people – literally thousands – with the travel bug.

Needless to say, I contracted one hefty dose of the travel bug myself, setting up my own specialised travel business for the traveller who wanted something, well, a bit different ... Prestige Stayathome Travel was designed to appeal to the executive who found himself too busy for a holiday. Instead, he found that Prestige Stayathome would bring travel to his sitting room: for a modest fee (negotiable) he would obtain the following:

- Sun-ray lamp (1)
- Foreign food: *either* pasta (spaghetti, etc) *or* Indian curry
- Video (1 hour) of foreign travel (Mexico or Scotland, as available)
- Paul Theroux in person (1 hour) with 5 anecdotes about loopy foreigners OR 5 sensitive reactions to foreign environments
- Piggyback rides from Sir Freddie Laker in person (extra)

Due to the rise in oil prices, Prestige Stayathome ceased trading in mid-1979. Win some, et cetera. The rest of that year I prepared for:

1980: The Error of Pop Videos

Being there at the birth of a new art form is something many dream of but few actually experience. I got into the biz by sheer chance: I used to have the odd drinkeroo in a dive in Swansea with a crazy guy called Mike who had once been in Lieutenant Pigeon (remember them?). Anyway, Mike and yours t. got talking, and it seems that he wanted to relaunch his career. 'Trouble is,' he confided, 'there's no one around who knows how to make a video.'

'I'm your man, Mikey,' I bluffed, and he took me on.

Poor guy had no idea I'd never made a video in my life!

But in less than a week, I'd learned all the tricks, hired a camera AND made a Video Classic – not bad, eh?

'Dreamin'' by Mike 'Lieutenant Pigeon' Pratt

VIDEO SCRIPT by Chris P. Rice

Produced and Directed by Chris P. Rice

Lyric: DREAMIN'. THAT'S WHAT I'M DOIN'
         I'M DREAMIN'

Video: We're in the middle of this vast empty ballroom with Mike singing in the centre
Lyric: DREAMIN'. THAT'S WHAT I'M DOIN'
I'M DREAMIN'
Video: Close-up of chandelier swinging in the wind
Lyric: DREAMIN' OF YOU LOVIN' ME GIRL
Video: Girl running towards camera in soft focus
Lyric: DREAMIN' OF HOW THINGS WERE LIKE
Video: Leaves blowing in the wind
Lyric: BEFORE THEY WERE LIKE WHAT THEY ARE LIKE NOW, GIRL
Video: Back to ballroom. Mike, anguished, in silhouette
Lyric: DREAMIN' OF WANTING THINGS TO BE MORE LIKE THEY WERE THEN THAN WHAT THEY ARE LIKE NOW JUST DREAMIN'
Video: Girl on horse riding along sandy beach in sunset
Lyric: DREAMIN'. THAT'S WHAT I'M DOIN'
I'M DREAMIN'
Video: Dream sequence: Mike in white room, dressed in white with white piano, girl on white horse enters, dressed all in white. It's all so white, they don't notice one another
Lyric: DREAMIN'. DREAMIN'. DREAMIN' (fade)
Running time 2 mins. 10 secs.

That took over a year to make. I learned something else: art takes time.

1982: The Error of the Great Trivia Boom

Frankly, I was a complete trivia nut years before it became fashionable.

Did you know that the average human body has passed through a glass of water at least eight times?

Amazing!

But true.

Did you know that the Golden Eagle spends most of his day reading the small print of *The Times* from eight miles up in the air?

Incredible!

But true.

Did you know that the average human being eats the most

tremendous amount of food over the course of his life, I can't remember how much exactly, but it's something really extraordinary – literally tons?

Unbelievable!

But true.

Did you know –

– You see, it's contagious!

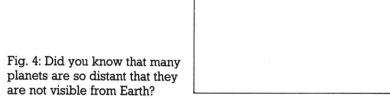

Fig. 4: Did you know that many planets are so distant that they are not visible from Earth?

So a pal of mine schlepped up to me and told me he knew a couple of fellow nutcases who were working on – yes, you got it – Trivial Pursuit, and would I like to write a few quezzies for said game?

You betcha, I intoned, just how trivial do you want?

Did you know that the fruit 'an orange' is so-called because, when ripe, it has an orange hue?

Did you know that the average human being spends literally years of his life asleep?

Did you know that the 'windmill' is powered solely by wind – hence the name?

Did you know that birds are almost the only animals in the world that have the ability to fly?

Did you know that dolphins can communicate with each other underwater?

Did you know that John Wayne's real name was not John Wayne?

Did you know that the sun is so hot that it is unlikely that man will ever be able to set foot on it?

Did you know that if you fold a piece of paper eight times it will become incredibly creased?

Did you know that, contrary to popular belief, the Eiffel Tower is situated in Paris, France?
Did you know – stop me, someone, it's contagious!!!

So I rattled off a list of 2000 utterly trivial facts for 'em, and I heard that they were thinking of using one or two, but that was years ago.

1984: The Error of Drying Out

Frankly, I'd overdone it.

To put it mildly.

Dope. Booze. Acid. Coke. You name it. Benzedrine. Hash. Smack. Dettol. Uppers. Downers. Omo. Haliborange. Speed. Dextrosol. You name it. Toblerone. Alka-Seltzer. Toffos. Smarties. Lucozade. Milk. And thick, thick chocolate. I'd inject or ingest anything that came to hand. Spoons. Cardboard. Flowers. Cushions. On one crazy occasion, a telephone receiver. In fact, it was when the telephone rang and I had to put my hand down my throat to answer it that I knew I had a Problem. I'd hit rock bottom and needed help.

So this was 1984. An Orwellian vision of a nightmarish hell. I realised then that I had to take a cool, calm look at myself and face up to some pretty terrifying Home Truths I'd spent the best part of my life avoiding. Please, don't call me courageous: I'm just a helluva lot more honest than most guys. Here's the list, and I don't care who reads it. Perhaps it'll be of help to someone out there.

Home Truths about Myself

1) I care too much for the feelings of others.
2) I just can't stop sticking up for the underdog.
3) I have to give, give, give: I find it hard to start taking.
4) I'm too intellectual for my own good.
5) I know it's wrong in this day and age, but I like people.

Not a very nice list to read about yourself, eh? But at least I now knew who I was. And this stood me in good stead for:

1985: The Error of the Style Magazine

Basically, we were going to have the best of everything: someone who used to know Richard Branson was pretty sure he could get Tom Wolfe to do something, and by all accounts Anthony Burgess was very interested in letting us have a specially-written piece and then of course we thought we'd approach Ted Hughes to be TV critic because someone said he was really keen on TV and a friend of a friend knew someone who knew Jorge Luis Borges's great friends, and it sounded as if we'd get Borges writing a style column on London street life. So there was a lot of interest all round.

Well, we didn't get absolutely everyone we wanted, that would have been too much to expect for the first issue. I mean, word hadn't got around yet, but we had some pretty exciting contributions all the same. People like

Julie Burchill on 'Brezhnev or Bee Gees: The East/West Debate'
Philip Howard on 'What a Lovely Old Language It Is'
Melvyn Bragg on 'The Novels of Melvyn Bragg'
Penny Perrick on 'Should Women Do All the Housework?'
Peregrine Worsthorne on 'Mrs Thatcher: Our Greatest Socialist'
Joanna Lumley on 'Look! I Can Write Too'
Jonathan Raban on 'What's Wrong With Me, Sorry, Make That What's Wrong With England'
Anne de Courcey on 'It's a Funny Old Life, 'cept When I Write About It'

Mainly because of the rise in the price of oil, *Escalator* folded after the first issue, but it was amazingly influential while it was going. Everyone said so.

1987: The Error of AIDS

It was a joke for a year, but now we know the truth.
Apparently, you can pick up AIDS just by talking to

someone who's talked about it within anything up to a week, well, that's what I heard on the radio anyway, and apparently the guy who interviewed the doctor is already undergoing treatment.

The thing is, I've been talking about it all year, but luckily I've never bothered to listen to what anyone else has said about it, so I'm all right. But apparently, there's this factory where they're making condoms for the head. The way it works is you cover your entire head with a condom and then you can talk about AIDS for however long you want with a partner of either sex. Apparently.

Fig. 5: There is no known cure for AIDS

Name

Terence de Brittish

Date of birth

Dec 25th, 1915

Profession

Newspaper Proprietor, Captain of Industry

Position currently held

Chairman, the *Daily Daily* and the *Sunday Daily* Newspaper Group

Family

Four children – Terence, Terencia, Terry and little Terrine, and a lovely female, Lady Clara de Brittish (née de Topliss) who has been my devoted wife for thirty-odd years.

Achievements to date

Creator of many ideas ahead of their time – the odour-free lightbulb, the ready-fried deep-frozen egg, lather-free soap, sound-only movies – all these were originally my ideas, but the Great British Public is so unwilling to welcome anything truly worthwhile that they never got off the ground. Thankfully, the *Daily Daily* and the *Sunday Daily*, my two super new newspapers, look like jogging them out of their complacency.

Awards

The Terence de Brittish Gold Oscar for Services to the Nation, 1967
– first ever recipient.
Many times nominated for a Knighthood.
Freeman of the city of Chernobyl, 1986.
Many times presented to the Royal Family.
Personal friend of Mrs Thatcher.

High point of career

Earning the respect and gratitude of the Great British Public and
the admiration of the international community for bringing the
Eurovision Song Contest to these shores, thus saving this
cherished institution from almost certain closure.

Low point of career

The turning-down of my application for Presidency of Guatemala in
1981: together we could have gone places and, I believe, still will.

Best friend

Many friends in the world of show-biz and politics inc. Anita Harris,
Freddie Raphael, Mark Thatcher, Gloria Hunniford and the people of
Ethiopia.

What makes you happy

Though a shy man, I like to stage large parties for all the lovely
people who have helped me over the years. In this respect, I am
often compared to The Great Glatsby. I like a bit of glamour, a bit of
razzamatazz: for instance, Norman Vaughan sometimes sings at
my do's.

What makes you sad

That men of calibre such as my young friend Mark Thatcher are driven out of the country to America, where they admire free enterprise.

What qualities do you look for in a human being

A man whose signature is his handshake.
A man with the ability to laugh at himself.
A man who is not too proud to say, 'Brittish, you're boss.'
A man who can stand up to me but does not feel the need to answer back.

Most memorable disaster

After my newspaper's admirable campaign to save the Ethiopian famine victims, I had the very great privilege of flying out the thirty sacks of grain donated by the Great British Public. Alas, half way over, I felt a bit peckish, and by the time we had landed there were only two and a bit sacks left. Luckily, the Ethiopians as a people are noted for their tremendous sense of humour.

Heroes

Dickie Mountbatten. One of nature's gentlemen. British as they come. Beautiful hands. Piercing blue eyes. Great respect for the young. Desperately worried by the rise of Soviet-trained agitators and subversives in the Commons. Marvellously soft skin.

Ambitions

I have always wanted a Top 10 hit and next Christmas I intend to cut a disc for my own record company, a cover version of Clive Dunn's 'Grandad', because that, I like to think, is how this great nation sees me – as everyone's wise old grandad whose name spells wisderm.

If you weren't yourself who would you choose to be

Someone with his whole life ahead of him. Mark Thatcher, for instance, is a lad of immense potential with a great future – and bags of charm.

Pets if any

A dog, Terence.

Hobbies

Scaletric, Meccano, model railway.

Religious convictions if any

Please consult my religious adviser.

Favourite book

The Old Curiosity Shopped by Geoffrey Dickens.

If you had three wishes what would they be

1. To have twenty more.
2. To sell each of those twenty for a 200–300 per cent profit.
3. To plough back 50 per cent of that profit into the development of more wishes.

What would you most like to be remembered for

Never promising anyone anything.
Being a man of my word.

Pet hate

Union officials who are so out of touch with their workforce that they think that management owes them a living.

Favourite catchphrase

There's no such word as Carn't.

Are you frightened of death and if so why

Luckily, my doctor tells me that I am not the dying type.

In Memory of
MY DEAR OLD MUM
May They Never Find Out Where She's Buried

'Money, Money, Money
It's so Sunny, Honey'

(from 'The Brilliant Mr de Brittish' by Chris
P. Rice, commissioned to celebrate sixty years
of purposeful and prosperous trading by
Terence de Brittish, 1987)

In 1929, I arrived in this great country of ours with only two shillings in my pocket and the suit I was standing up in.

Just two years later, in 1929, I had more than doubled that original two shillings. I now had five shillings in my pocket. By astute financial dealing, I had sold the suit I had stood up in for that extra three shillings, whilst retaining overall control of the pocket.

And it did not stop there.

By 1932 I possessed 100 per cent of half a pair of shoes. I had cut down the unnecessary excess on my gross capital, and with the slimmer, more energetic and easily manageable sum of two pence in my half-pocket I felt ready to take on the world.

It was in the cut-and-thrust years of the thirties that I developed my three golden rules of business:

- Never Say No To A Cup Of Tea
- No Problem Is So Big That It Cannot Be Ignored
- Things Can Only Get Better

By 1938, I was worth well over ten shillings. I had arrived in Fleet Street. After a number of false starts, I had hit upon the idea of applying for a railway timetable – a rash move, you might think – but it worked. I had left Eastbourne on the 8.14, and arrived in Fleet Street at 10.35.

With the onset of the war, I put business interests to one side.

In times of crisis, my country will always come first with me.

In 1946, I arrived back in this great country of ours with only two shillings in my pocket and the suit I was standing up in.

It was around this time that I met my future wife, Lady Clara de Topliss, worth at that time over 6 million pounds – in those days, a lot of money.

It was love at first sight.

People often ask me whether it was a disadvantage marrying someone so rich. Not at all, I always reply – I take people as I see them. Just ten years later, by 1957, through astute wheeler-dealing coupled with a sharp business sense, I had multiplied her original 6 million pounds into 4½ million pounds – without the bank owing us a penny.

The rest, as they say, is history. I wine and dine with the best.

Along the way, I've picked up a secret or two about how to run a successful business. Never Borrow More Than You Can Spend. Sell At A Loss, Buy For More Than You Bargained For. Money Isn't Everything. These hints will take you to the Top. But one rule has governed all my business life –

RULE 1: **THERE'S NO SUCH WORD AS CARN'T**

When a business acquaintance says something to you, wait a few seconds before giving him a reply.

In those few seconds, you must think like you've never thunk before.

Business acquaintance: *How are you keeping, Terence de Brittish?*

A seemingly innocuous question. Nothing wrong there, you might think. But stop.

Ask yourself *the three W's:*

WHAT does he mean?
(Keeping – odd word to employ. Does he believe me to be harbouring something that I am not admitting to? Something illegal perhaps? And why should he believe this? Is it true? Are a lot of people thinking this about me? How did the rumour start? Who's been telling them these things? Why did he include my name in the question? Did he think I might be someone else? Has he seen through my alias? Do I have an alias? Why do I have an alias if I do? Did he really say 'How' or

did I mishear him say 'Who'? Does he think I'm keeping someone? Perhaps without their permission, against their will? Is it true? What can he want?)

WHEN does he want a final answer?
(Is he putting me on the spot? If I don't reply straightaway, will he think I've got something to hide? Why shouldn't I reply straightaway? Have I got something to hide? Could I post him the reply under plain cover? And why under plain cover?)

WHERE is he?
(Is he standing opposite me now? Does he have eye-contact with me? How can I tell? I mean, really tell? If it is him, why's he there? Why isn't he somewhere else? If I'm the most important person he could think of to deal with, shouldn't I be with someone more important?)

But above all APPEAR UNFLUSTERED. If he suspects for one second that you have something to hide, he'll find you out.

After a few seconds thought, speak loudly and firmly, so that you can be easily heard:

Terence de Brittish: *I am keeping very well thank you.*
Then pause for half a second before adding:
Terence de Brittish: *And how are you keeping yourself?*
The ball is now in his court. You have successfully parried his initial thrust, and it's him who's now in the deep end.
Business acquaintance: *Not too bad myself thanks.*
Remember: Ask yourself those Three W's – What, When, Where? But while you pause, he has already cut in with:
Business acquaintance: *Weather's not so good today though is it?*
Remember once again those Three W's. But he's cut in again before you've had a chance to riposte.
Business acquaintance: *I'm told rain is expected.*
Remember again those Thr –
Business acquaintance: *That's what they're saying anyway.*
Remem –
Business acquaintance: *Not that they're ever right are they ha ha!*

Your business acquaintance has finally relinquished his position as INSTIGATOR, having ended his last remark with a QUESTION (Are they?) and leaving it up to you to supply an ANSWER. But the QUESTION is TECHNICAL in this case, demanding some KNOWLEDGE of the expertise or otherwise of the weather commentators. This is when

RULE 2: **NEVER BE WRONG**

comes into play. If you do not know with CERTAINTY the TECHNICAL JUDGEMENT that you are being challenged to IMPART then do not be drawn into the debate or your business reputation will suffer. Instead say:

Terence de Brittish: *I have never gone into the matter fully enough to be able to come up with a positive answer to that one so if you'll forgive me I'll defer judgement.*
But then, before your business acquaintance can get a word in –
Business acquaintance: *Ah well, mustn't gr –*
you must take stock of the situation and make your move for the UPPER HAND with a far-reaching QUESTION he must answer at length:
Terence de Brittish: *Now tell me a little bit about yourself.*
and while he falls into your pre-set trap, you now have TIME TO PLAY WITH. As his answer rambles on, ask yourself the essential questions every successful businessman has on the tip of his fingers:

Business acquaintance: *Well to be honest with you Terence de*
Terence de Brittish: thinks: a) What is he selling? b) What am *Brittish I'm a bit of a risk-taker well you have to be in this business* I buying? c) Is what he is selling worth me buying? d) If I *don't you there's no time for standing still but early on in my* buy what he is selling will there be someone to buy it? e) Will *business career I realised that if you could minimise risk maximise* the person who buys what he has sold and I have bought be *output and marbelise your main entrance hall then you more than* able to sell it? f) Is he trying to blind me with difficult jargon? *likely had an odds-on chance of going somewhere and being* g) Does he think that I am more stupid than he is? h) Am I

something not just one of the crowd well you have to in this business
more stupid than he is? i) If I am more stupid than he is, how
don't you so I started off in commodities yes I'm really a
can I make him think that he's more stupid than I am? j) Or
commodities man sugar oil motor vehicles fruit heavy plant you
isn't he that stupid? k) If he is more stupid than I am why did
name it but then I branched into conceptualised market strategies
they send him to deal with me? l) Do they think I'm stupid?
coming swiftly to the conclusion that in this day and age in this
m) If he's more clever than me why did they send him to deal
day and age you've got to think on your feet or you're out on your
with me? n) They think I'm stupid – they do, well I'll bloody
uppers well that's what I always say.
show them who's stupid around here.

Now that you have assessed the situation, exercise your GET
OUT CLAUSE with the decisive statement:

Terence de Brittish: *Lovely to have met you. Nice to have got to
know you. Must meet again soon. If you'll forgive me I am in
a meeting but will call back later let's have lunch!*

Without a further word exercise your Masonic handshake.
This will tell him all he wants to know and nothing you don't
want him to know. Of course, this can only be truly operational
if you obey:

RULE 3: JOIN THE FREEMASONS, MAKE A LOT OF LOVELY FRIENDS, HELP DESERVING CHARITIES, AND FURTHER YOUR BUSINESS INTERESTS

You will always recognise a fellow freemason by his parting
remark:

'LET'S HAVE LUNCH!'

and by his handshake, which can mean a variety of things.

a) Pressure applied to 1st Knuckle: 'What are you drinking?'

b) Pressure applied to 2nd Knuckle: 'I wouldn't say no to a pink gin'

c) Pressure applied to 3rd Knuckle: 'I accept American Express'

d) Pressure applied to 4th Knuckle: 'I am the Duke of Kent'

e) Pressure applied to 1st and 3rd Knuckles simultaneously: 'I fancy you something rotten'

f) Pressure applied to 2nd and 4th Knuckles simultaneously: 'But I am the Commissioner of the Metropolitan Police. It is out of the question'

g) Pressure not applied at all: 'Your knee is still showing'

h) Pressure applied to 6th Knuckle: 'Hey! You've got six fingers!'

i) Pressure applied to inside pocket: 'Pray excuse me while I steal your wallet'

To my mind, a lot of guff and nonsense has been written about Freemasonry by journalists and similar oddballs. It is a Christian Businessmen's Association and takes a free-market economy theological approach to Christ's teachings, while adhering rigidly to an adaptation of the Ten Commandments more suited to the consumer-orientated society we live in today.

1) Thou Shalt Not Kill
2) Thou Shalt Not Steal
3) Thou Shalt Not Commit Adultery
4) The Customer Is Always Right
5) Thou Shalt Not Covet Thy Neighbour's Wife
6) Trespassers Will Be Prosecuted
7) Sit Well Back In Your Seat For Safety And Comfort
8) Thou Shalt Not Worship Graven Images
9) Duck Or Grouse
10) You Don't Have To Be Mad To Work Here – But It Helps

These are the maxims by which we strive to live our lives. Nothing sinister, I think you'll agree. And then there are our extraordinarily wide-reaching charity organisations, the Worshipful Order of the Ferret, the All-Stars Backhanders Cricketing XI, the Old Corpulents and the Grand Lodge of Petulant Crisp Manufacturers. 90 per cent of this country's High Court judges, many of whom I've had the pleasure to do business with, wouldn't care to be mixed up with anything remotely 'sinister'. Point taken?

RULE 4: THE FIRST THING IS TO DECIDE WHAT YOU'RE TRYING TO DO. YOU THEN DECIDE HOW YOU'RE GOING TO GO ABOUT DOING IT. NEXT YOU DO IT. THEN YOU LOOK AT WHAT YOU HAVE DONE. WHY DIDN'T IT WORK? YOU TELL ME.

My good friend Max Bygraves, that great all-round family entertainer, and not a bad golfer to boot, is fond of starting his hilarious yarns with the words, 'Let me tell you a story'. Well, if Max can do it, so can a leading Captain of Industry.

Let me tell you a story.

By the end of 1971, due solely to the intransigence of the dead weight of tradition hanging over British industry and the crippling demands of the trade unions I finally had to close my two highly modern pioneering newspapers, *The New Daily*

Australasia and Far East Late Sports and Weather News and its companion paper, *The New Sunday Daily Australasia and Far East Late Sports and Weather News*. Both had failed to catch on in Dorking, their sole distribution area. It was a painful decision having to sack my entire workforce, but they shared my delight that I had managed to retain my country seat, Brittish Building, and my three runaround helicopters.

RULE 5: THE MAN WHO INSPIRES LOYALTY IN HIS WORKFORCE WILL FIND IT EASIER TO GET RID OF THEM IN THE LONG RUN

But I was in a hell of a position. I owed my banks half a million. I had virtually no resources. People were muttering that I was a broken man. So what did I do?

I sat down and thank.

When I stood up again, I had conceived and planned a revolution.

Casebook: The Daily and Sunday Daily
Of the three schemes that came into my head that bleak November morning, my new dream for a national daily and Sunday newspaper seemed the least likely to succeed.

Yet today the *Daily Daily* and the *Sunday Daily* are regularly bought by a combined total of over 375 people.

RULE 6: NOTICE A GAPING HOLE IN THE MARKET AND STEP INTO IT

For some time now, I had been dissatisfied with the coverage I was getting from the regular newspapers produced daily by the barons in their ivory towers, no names, no pack drill!

They gave me murders; they gave me royalty; they gave me any other news there might be; they gave me sports; they gave me the arts (books etc); they gave me weather; they gave me television; they gave me dolly birds; they gave me entertainment; they gave me cartoons.

But that left a huge gaping hole.

It seemed so obvious, I couldn't believe that no one else had ever thought of it. Amazing.

But true.

Normal news.

It came to me like a bolt from heaven – not a single national newspaper gave any attention to the dull and normal things which form the essence of all of our lives.

They'd tell us about a mass murder that happened over ten thousand miles from our front door, but they'd tell us nothing whatever about our doormat.

They'd tell us about a change of government in China, but they'd tell us nothing whatever about a change of sheets at home.

They'd tell us about typhoons and earthquakes in Mexico, but it might be quite sunny outside our own home and we'd never get to hear of it.

How many members of the Royal Family are there alive today? Nine? Ten? Possibly eleven? And yet how many ordinary people are there who never appear in our national press? Millions.

I became convinced that a newspaper that told its readers exactly as it is – normal – would prove a knockout success. And I wasn't wrong.

RULE 7: **PEOPLE WILL BUY WHAT THEY WANT TO BUY IF THEY CAN AFFORD IT**

Casebook: Marketing, Distribution and Sales Report

For Day One, we aimed at a world exclusive – and sure enough we got it. The very first edition of the *Daily Daily* carried the banner headline:

MOST PEOPLE GOT
OUT OF BED
THIS MORNING!

The story that followed alerted readers to the fact that they, like many others, had neither died in their sleep nor caught a chill, but had woken up and got out of bed successfully. A diagram with arrows demonstrated the process of 'getting out of bed'. Here was a human normality story with which all readers could identify.

Other pages kept up the pace:

BIRD EATS WORM!

FARMER MAKES CUP OF NESCAFÉ!

TAXI DRIVER TAKES LUNCH BREAK!

NO ONE RAPED IN BASINGSTOKE!

SLIGHT DRIZZLE IN SHEFFIELD!

All these normal stories combined to make our first edition a brilliant success – and we had our royal exclusive too –

QUEEN SHAKES HAND!

The newspaper surpassed all our dreams. On new technology, we printed our 500,000 expecting to sell 350,000 and in fact sold 12, which was short of our target but immensely encouraging in the long run. Nothing is more dangerous than peaking too early. I might add that our marketing wizards estimate for potential advertisers that each issue of the *Daily Daily* is in fact read by up to 1000 readers per copy. After six months, we are keeping sales steady, whilst other national dailies have noticed sharp declines in circulation following the initial launch. But one must never be too complacent.

RULE 8: **NEVER SIT BACK OR YOUR CHAIR WILL COLLAPSE**

Casebook: My Present Project
Any sound businessman will tell you that there is a lot of money in food. Take one look inside a restaurant and you will see everybody eating the stuff.

But we have been trained by society to eat only some food – lamb, beef, pork and so on.

Funny how inspiration strikes. I was looking at a rat in a gutter one day, great big beast it was, lot of flesh on it, when I thought to myself:

I CAN SEE THAT ON A PLATE WITH A BIT OF GRAVY

Immediately, I got my experts working on a Boil-in-the-Bag Rat at a price attractive to the general housewife. They came up with a marketing man's dream – fillet of rat in a Mornay sauce with wild rice, less than 350 calories, all for £1.95. A sure-fire winner, I was told. But there were hazards ahead.

Casebook: Boil-in-the-Bag Low-Calorie Rat Mornay and Wild Rice
Our tests showed that there was nothing wrong with the product, nothing at all.

It tasted good.

It was priced competitively.

It was beautifully packaged.

Yet it came up against almost 100 per cent consumer reluctance.

Believe it or not, but your average housewife, bless her cotton socks, was put off by that little word 'rat'. Hard to credit – but true. Seems they associated 'rat' not with chunky morsels of succulent beef-style meat but with disease, vermin and sewers.

RULE 9: **IT DOESN'T MATTER IF THE PUBLIC THINKS YOUR PRODUCT'S DISGUSTING – THEY WILL BUY IT ANYWAY**

At the moment, my marketing boys are going flat out to improve the image of rat. We've hired some of the most attractive rats to pose with a small group of spring lambs. We've organised that Liz Taylor's next marriage but one will be to a well-connected rat. Chris P. Rice has written a catchy jingle to let the world know that there's nothing tastier than a rat:

Head – Body – Tail!
Head – Body – Tail!
Yummy-Yummy-Yummy!
There something in a Rat
For Mum, Dad and Kiddy!
And it's dead before it reaches your Tummy!

VOICEOVER: RAT. DEAD BEFORE IT REACHES YOUR TUMMY.

To put the final seal of success on the op, I have agreed to appear in plus-fours and deerstalker kit at the front door of my country seat surrounded by fifty Rat-in-a-Bag factory staff, all dressed as yokels and waving fifty rats by the tail. After they have finished cheerin' and wavin', the camera focuses on me (and may I say at this juncture that I eschew personal publicity) and I give a right beamin' smile and say endearingly:

'Rats – they're vermin' delicious!'

A sure-fire winner, my marketing boys assure me.

May I Bend Your Ear?

By now, you're probably thinking you'd like to be like me. Rich. Powerful. Helicopter, wife, four beautiful kids and a fleet of smart cars. Well respected by the international community. And much loved.

But one thing seems to stand in your way.

You can't make head or tail of what the boffins call 'economics'.

My advice? Ignore the eggheads. They dress simple common sense up in a lot of fancy verbiage so as to keep you or me out of the trough.

Once you've seen through the economic jargon, you're on your way to your first hundred thou.

D'you honestly think that a successful young businessman like Mark Thatcher knows his upturn from his indices?

'Course he doesn't. And that's because he's read:

THE DE BRITTISH A–Z OF ECONOMIC JARGON

A   **Above Board.** Not yet legislated against.
B   **Brave Initiative.** Futile face-saver.
C   **Consultant.** Nob with handle.
D   **Diversify.** Clear out.
E   **Energetic.** Restless.
F   **Further discussion necessary.** Piss off.
G   **Go-getter.** Ex-jailbird.
H   **High-profile.** Publicity-obsessed.
I   **Interest-free loan.** Backhander.
J   **Job satisfaction.** Low paid but uncomplaining.
K   **Knighthood.** c/o Smith Square. Please enclose invoice.
L   **Law-abiding.** Unimaginative.
M   **Miracle recovery.** Soon to go under.
N   **No-nonsense.** Cheap.
O   **Opera.** High-profile image-builder, but noisy.
P   **Potential.** Failure so far.
Q   **Quality control.** Man with the tube of glue.
R   **Rosy future.** Better off gardening.
S   **Safe.** No return.
T   **Tried and tested.** And failed on all counts.
U   **Upmarket.** Overpriced.
V   **Valued customer.** No money to spend.
W   **Whizz kid.** Crook approaching fifty.
X   **X.** Sign here, skip the small print.
Y   **Yours.** Soon mine.
Z   **Zzzzzz.** Fruitful working lunch.

Name

Ambrose de Solaire

Date of birth

Year of the Cockroach

Profession

Mind Researcher, Company Director

Position currently held

Mind-in-Chief, Universal Insight Limited

Family

of Man

Achievements to date

1966, Founder and Editor *Purple Haze* magazine; 1967, Founder and Chancellor of University of Perfect Truth, California; 1968, Road Manager to Allen Ginsberg; later same year, placed acid in water-supply of self; 1969, three days of love and peace at Woodstock Festival, Woodstock, the World; 1970, Organiser, International Frisbee Convention, Milwaukee; 1971, volunteered, defence witness 'Oz' trials – not called; 1972–74, journey to India in search of Paul McCartney who is dead; 1975–86, Founded UIL Worldwide International Inc. Expand own mind and others.

Awards

Donor and Recipient of first ever Spiritual Excellence Award, first class, 1983.

High point of career

Shook hands with John Lennon, New York, 1979.

Low point of career

All experience of this life is worthwhile, everything.

Best friend

Squaw Running Flower, my ancient Egyptian alter ego and mentor.

What makes you happy

Self-knowledge.
Freak-outs.

What makes you sad

Turmoil, inner and outer.
Wealth.
Freak-outs.

What qualities do you look for in a human being

green
pink
purple
liquid

Most memorable disaster

American invasion of Vietnam.

Heroes

Max D. Stanfield. You won't have heard of him, but he was a tramp I met in a New York subway in 1967. A man with inner karma and great gentleness: to me, a hero.
Bernard Levin.

Ambitions

To know myself better, and maybe to go away for a weekend or two with myself.

If you weren't yourself who would you choose to be

A butterfly.
A letter in a word written by Bernard Levin.

Pets if any

A goldfish called Penis. What's wrong with that? It's a beautiful word describing a beautiful part of the body.

Hobbies

Frisbee.
Tie-dye.
Enlightenment.
Overturning capitalism by making money.
Watching old videos of *The Flintstones* (they're cartoons and not real people – FACT).

Religious convictions if any

Do you have a year or five to spare? Briefly – and remember I've been studying this subject for over half my life – the world is a globe, and so is the skull of a man. A round bowl full of water is also a globe, and so is a ball which bounces. A bowl; a ball; a skull; the globe. We have to make connections between them before the Truth is revealed.

Favourite book

Anything with the Flintstones or Gurdjieff in it.
Anything by McLuhan.
Anything by Bernard Levin.
Anything deep with or without pictures.

If you had three wishes what would they be

1. To lose myself
2. By losing myself, to find myself
3. To lose myself again

What would you most like to be remembered for

My rule of life: No Island Is a Man.

Pet hate

I prefer the word aversion. I try to see the good in everything.

Favourite catchphrase

The spade which is never used digs deepest.

Are you frightened of death and if so why

No.
I am to be reborn as EITHER a sweet-pea or the first World President.

Are you as paranoid as they say you are?

Please apply your mind to the following questionnaire.
Suggested time: One hour and a half.

1)  A ⬜ B

a) Is a square.
b) Is a circle.

QUESTION: Do you agree with the above statements (a) and (b)?
YES/NO

If your answer is No please abandon this questionnaire now.
You are wasting our time. You have no intention of opening
your mind to those powers beyond your own paltry human
reason. You do not wish to discover the unknown. Clear off.
If your answer is Yes you have done very well. You have
gained 3000 (three thousand) points. We are so glad you have
decided to join us. We'd like to hug you if we may. Welcome
friend. Lovely to have you among us.

2) What sort of fish are you?

a) A goldfish   **b)** A crab   **c)** A salmon

A/B/C

All fish are beautiful, so be delighted in your choice.
Nevertheless, this helps our experts establish particulars about
your character and personality, and these particulars will help
us in fitting you into our UIL programme. If you are a goldfish,
you will be working in the kitchens; if you are a crab, you will
be in charge of waste disposal; if you are a salmon you are too
obsessed with power and must allow your ego to diminish by
scrubbing floors.

3) Please cut off your small toe. Into which box does it fit?

A/B/C/D

If your severed toe is now lying in one of the above boxes, you are an essentially submissive character with little pride in your own body. You may well not be suitable for our UIL course.

4) You are a bird flying high in the sky. Like Jonathan Livingston Seagull, you have found freedom: you have found yourself. From a mile above the ground, you finish reading the small print of *The Times* then swoop down low above a rushing brook. There you see a small fish that has lost its mother in a drowning accident. The fish has been befriended by a sheepdog, and is taking rides on the sheepdog's back. Elsewhere in the meadow, a butterfly, chancing upon the goldfish riding upon the sheepdog's back, flickers and flutters so that he may ride on the back of the goldfish. See the cheery confederates as they rollick across the meadow. You, the bird, hover low, caressing the butterfly's wings with your own in a gesture of mutual respect. Suddenly a bull appears at the far end of the meadow: you suspect he may be an enemy, but, on looking at him again, you detect a certain warmth in those weary old eyes. 'Hey, Mr Bull!' you shout in your birdy-language. 'Come and join us frolicking in this meadow!' Up he jumps, landing on you, who lands on the butterfly, who lands on the fish, who lands on the dog. 'I thought you said we were frolicking,' says Mr Bull glumly.

QUESTION: What does this fable tell us?

a) That George Harrison was right when he said,
   'Truth, lovely, lovely, lovely Truth
   Sha la la, Sha la la, Truth
   And Light too, lovely, lovely, lovely Light
   Sha la la, Truth and Light, Sha la la'

b) That Paul McCartney was right when he said:

'Life's a silly nursery rhyme
So all the kiddies say
Aunty Flos and Uncle Jim
Way-Hay-Hay! Way-Hay-Hay!
(*chorus*) *So let's rock 'n' roll*
In Happy Land
And I'd love to join you.
But I just sacked the band
Way-Hay-Hay! Way-Hay-Hay!'

c) That Ringo Starr was right when he said:

'Brrroooommm! Brrrroooooommm!
Brrrooooooommmmm! Brrrrroooooooommmm!
Brrrrroooooommmmmm! Brrrrooooooommmm!
Blimey, I thought someone said this
Was a sports car and now I find it's
A drum-set.'

d) That John Lennon was right when he said:

'Imagine all the people
Living life in peas
Even if they were very small
They'd still have to bend their knees'

A/B/C/D

Each has its own truth. As Lennon said in another context, 'Everything is true – I wanna make love to you.'

5)

QUESTION: Do you see

a) Nothing at all
b) Just a blank piece of paper
c) Psychedelic dragons in fiery glades watching over dark dungeons
d) Heavy snow

A/B/C/D

The correct answer is (c) but do not be worried if you cannot yet see them. The purpose of UIL is to extend the imagination to encompass visions that are not readily available to those human beings stuck within the confines of Western materialist culture. After even 48 hours of the course, you will begin to see small things in that space – non-flowering shrubs, a piece of unbuttered toast, a page of the *Daily Telegraph* – and after a few more sessions your visions may well rise to the level of a dolphinarium, an open-top bus or a cross-channel ferry. Only to those who have been with UIL a long, long time is it given to see the psychedelic dragons.

6) Which of these is your favourite number:

A   9   B   7   C   413   D   0

A/B/C/D

None of these answers is 'correct'. It is high time you shook off Western materialist and individualist notions of winning and losing. They are all lovely numbers, good in themselves, useful for a multitude of different purposes, all of them essential for a rich and satisfying journey to self-knowledge. 'I am you and you are me and we are they and they are us and us are him and they are mine so get your own' ('Glass Onion' by John Winston Lennon).

But each number has a personal significance. Let us examine that significance – but remember, there is no 'right' or 'wrong'.

a) 9

If 9 is your favourite number, your gifts do not lie within your body or your intellect, but you have a lot to give others.

You will never be a leader, but will find solace in your willingness to serve.

Your conversation is dull in the extreme, but this is good: it allows you to listen to others.

You have been blessed with a body that is unattractive to your fellow human beings: this will help you to concentrate on the affairs of the mind and of the heart.

Avoid anything appertaining to the mind as others far excel you in this capacity.

You must devote yourself to the expansion of your heart, living your life on behalf of others, serving them and obeying all their commands.

You are beautiful.

Fellow UIL members who appreciate the number 9: Andrew Ridgeley, Benny Hawkins from *Crossroads*, Ann Parkinson, Mr Victoria Gillick, Mark Thatcher, Barney Rubble, Mark Phillips, Gerald Priestland, Jimmy Carter, Arianna Stassinopoulos, Gaye Gambol, Susan Hill, Mrs Betty Kenward

b) 7

If you have chosen 7, you are not someone who has the burden of originality to overcome. Up to 90 per cent of adults at any one time choose the number 7 as their particular favourite, and 85 per cent of this number are surprised that anyone else at all has chosen it for themselves.

You are insecure, finding comfort in convention and in 'fitting in'.

Your ambition is that things don't get any worse; your sexual fantasy is of a dinner for two with pleasant cabaret; when you dream, you imagine yourself asleep in bed, dreaming.

You will find out much about yourself on the UIL course and you will be surprised how much like Meg Mortimer in TV's long-running serial *Crossroads* you are, even though you are not dead.

You are beautiful because you are pliable.

You are a child of the Universe: you have a right to be here as long as you are accompanied by an adult.

Fellow UIL members who appreciate the number 7: Alan Coren, all the presenters of *Blue Peter*, Russell Davies, Felicity Kendal, Roger Moore, Jimmy Greaves, Sir Robert Mark, Tintin, Lord Whitelaw

c) 413

You think you are very original choosing the most peculiar number, but you are not. In tests, over 25 per cent of monkeys who expressed a preference chose the number 413. For some time now, you have believed yourself to be different from everyone else, superior even. You employ small gestures to show this to yourself and to the world:

   (i)   you go to films with subtitles
   (ii)   you sometimes wear a bow tie
  (iii)   you profess never to have watched *Dallas*
  (iv)   you sometimes don't read the newspapers
   (v)   you intimate that you have a drink problem, or could have if you tried hard enough

You are lower than the low.

You will only really know yourself when you have become someone completely different, someone who understands himself to be a nobody.

You are a meaningless piece of gristle.

But you are a beautiful meaningless piece of gristle, and we would like to welcome you to UIL.

Fellow UIL members who appreciate the number 413: Bernard Levin, Chris P. Rice, Clive James, Bill Wyman, Gloria Hunniford, Maureen Lipman, Lady Eva de Topliss, Madame Castafiore, Paul Daniels, Frederic Raphael, Lady Penelope, Hermione Lee

d) 0

You are a very negative individual. You care for no one and no one cares for you. You are only half alive.

You do not like giving; you do not even like taking.

When you wake up in the morning your first action is to go back to sleep.

You do not bother to listen to the weather forecast.

You leave things on the side of your plate not because you particularly disliked them but because you don't particularly like the plate.

You are a void, an empty hole, a nothing person. The only music you like has Julian Lloyd Webber in it somewhere and you only like films you have seen before.

You suspect your parents didn't like you, when to the rest of us it seems perfectly obvious that they didn't.

You will respond well to UIL. Soon that hole will be filled.

You have an immense capacity to receive, if only you knew it.
You are beautiful, what little there is of you.
Open your mind and let the sun shine in.

Fellow UIL members who appreciate the number 0: Richard Baker, Captain Scarlett, Stewart de Stuart, Miriam Stoppard, Wincey Willis, Angela Rumbold MP, Roger Scruton, Leonard Nimoy, Alf Roberts, Professor Calculus, Harold Pinter, Craig de Brown, Edward de Bono, Justin de Villeneuve

7) Study this picture carefully:

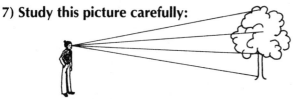

What do you think it portrays:

a) An artist viewing a tree in search of points of perspective
b) A farmer viewing a tree in search of squirrels
c) A tree-surgeon viewing a tree in search of disease

A/B/C

None of these is correct. You have little awareness of the impending threat in the natural world around you. The picture shows four snipers hiding in an oak tree shooting an innocent victim in the eyes. Nice, eh?

8) Look at this shape carefully:

Does it suggest to you:

a) A bed
b) Weightlifting weights
c) Two short lines connected by a third, longer, line
d) A rugby post

A/B/C/I

None of these answers remotely touch on the truth. It is in fact a half-painted tennis court seen from the air by an eagle. Your level of spiritual awareness is low and would greatly benefit from UIL.

9) Now stare long and hard at the palm of your Right Hand.

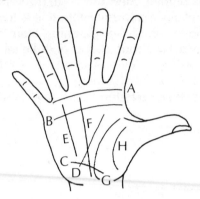

Frankly, it doesn't look too good, does it?

You are an outsider, someone who does not fit in, someone who is shunned by others. And with reason.

You have an extra finger. Ugh!

Let's take a closer look.

Line A is a scratch. You should have it looked at.

Line B is your Heart line. No one has ever loved you really, have they?

Line C is your Health line. Note its downward slant.

Line D is your Head line. It shows no brain-power. You are either: a) a woodpecker or b) Andrew Ridgeley.

Line E is a Biro mark. You are filthy.

Line F is your Life line, your Line of Destiny. Put it this way: if this was 1957, you would still have thirty years to live.

Line G is your Love line. It will be better for everyone if you remain a virgin.

Line H is your Status line. Were you once quite good at ice-skating?

How did you do?

Do not be disheartened if you scored low, or if, during the course of the 'test', you discovered some highly unpleasant truths about yourself. They have been festering away for many years in the dustbin of your mind: far better for everyone that they are now brought out and placed on the table. Here are a few more facts about yourself you never fully faced up to:

1) People find you a bit of a bore
2) *I* find you a bit of a bore, and I've never met you
3) People don't say really intelligent things to you because they think you wouldn't understand them
4) If you really think about it, you're not happy at all
5) You're not nearly as nice as some people think you are
6) People dread you ringing them up
7) All the waiters laugh behind your back, and so do your parents
   Your best friend does too
   Oh, and also that person you fancy
8) You spend quite a lot of time trying to concentrate for long enough to be able to think whether you believe in God or not and all the time God couldn't care less whether you do or you don't
9) All the time you have imagined people haven't noticed it, they haven't been able to stop thinking about it, and that's the way you're remembered by most people, even strangers. And don't pretend you don't know what I'm talking about
10) Deep down, you hate women
11) Deep down, you hate men
12) Actually, you have no sense of humour
13) God made you to contradict the human belief that all human life is sacred
14) When people nod in agreement with you it just means that they haven't bothered to hear what you said
15) You used to be more fun than you are now, but not much
16) You haven't really understood anything you've ever read
17) There's always been something a bit *odd* about you, but only a bit
18) Whenever you're in a room with people all they can think about is watching television
19) You have body odour
20) Even if you wash, you'll still have it
21) Not many years now and you'll be dead. Not many years after that and everyone will have forgotten you

YOU ARE NOW DRAINED OF ALL DESTRUCTIVE EGOTISM

YOU FEEL SUICIDAL, AND RIGHTLY SO

YOU ARE AN EMPTY CUP

PREPARE TO BE FILLED

Repeat this Mantra throughout the day and night until you have given your all and your bank cancels all standing orders

MANTRA

Food cannot be eaten by the ankle
Give Me Your Money

Love is a bird with three wings
I Said Give Me Your Money

Even the strongest swimmer cannot fly
All of It And Fast

Green is more green than red
Cheque Or Postal Order I Said Fast

Love is a box with no bottom, no top, no sides
Made Out To UIL Worldwide International Inc.

The fish that cannot swim must learn to walk

As you read these short prose-poems, these word-pictures, remember to breathe in and to breathe out: this process will aid your new living skills, allowing air to course through both body and brain. Slowly, slowly, you are learning rebirth.

WELCOME